Bond

No.1 for exam success

AF765124

Non-verbal Reasoning

10 Minute Tests

10–11^{+} years

OXFORD
UNIVERSITY PRESS

Test 1: Sequences and Codes

Test time: 0 5 10 minutes

Which pattern continues or completes the given series?

Example

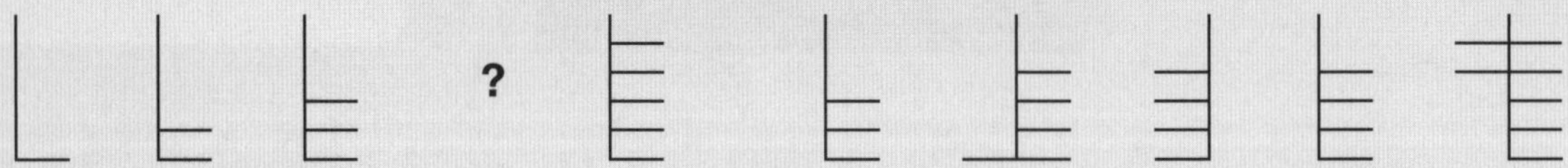

a b c (d) e

1

a b c d e

2

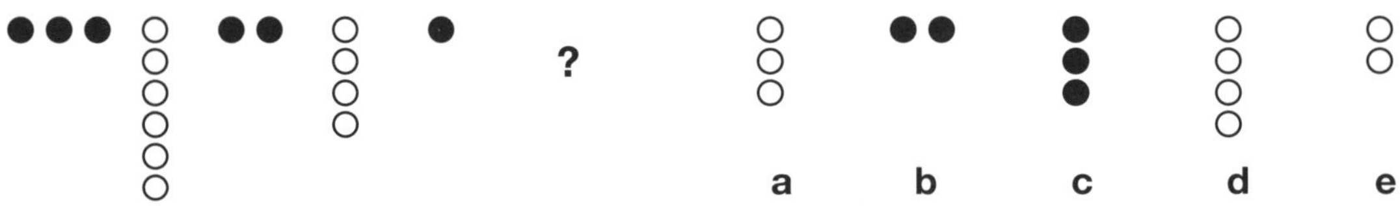

a b c d e

3

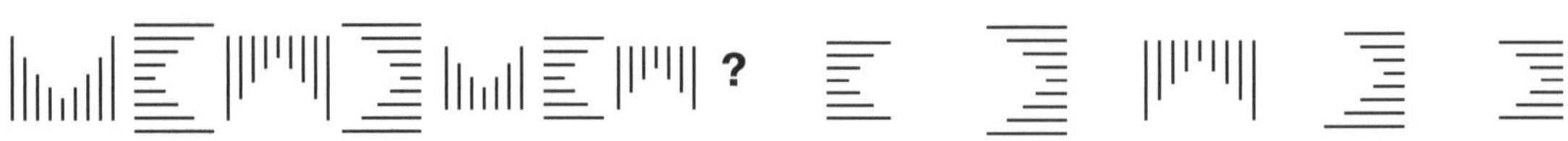

a b c d e

4

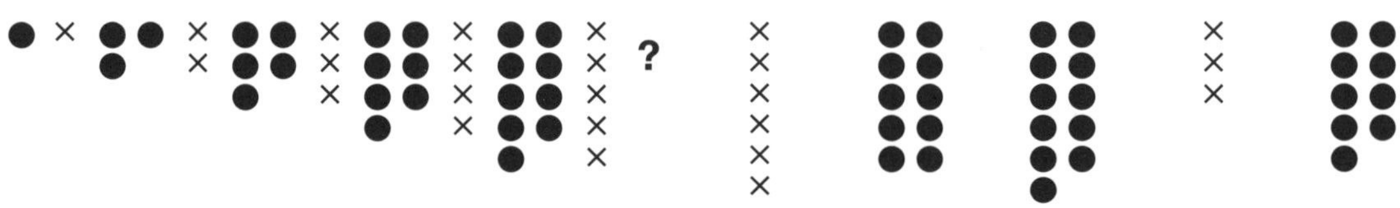

a b c d e

5

a b c d e

6

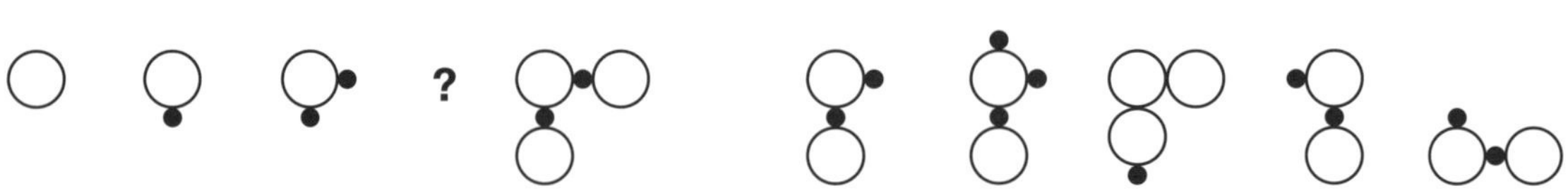

a b c d e

Using the given patterns and codes, select the code that matches the last pattern.

Example

AX AY BZ CY BX ?

AY AX CZ BZ BY
a b (c) d e

7

AD AE CE BF ?

AF BE CF CD BD
a b c d e

8

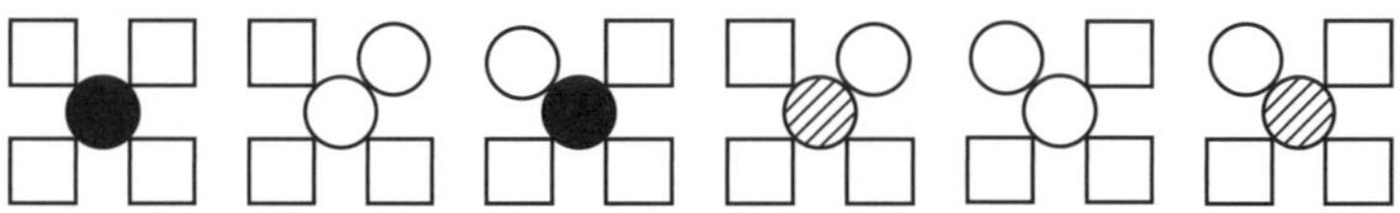

GZ HX JZ HY JX ?

JY JX HZ HY GY
a b c d e

9

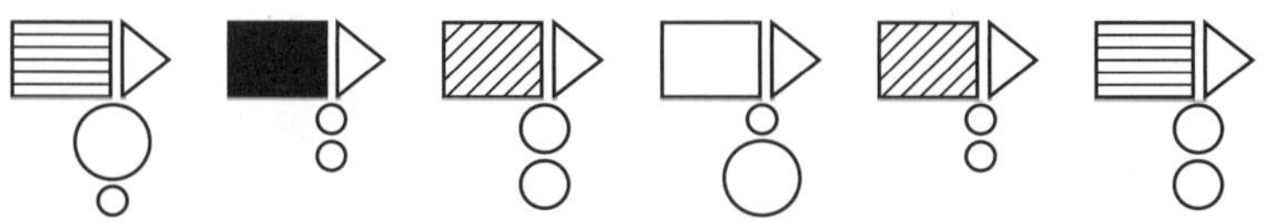

NW PY MV LX MY ?

PX LY NV MW PV
a b c d e

10

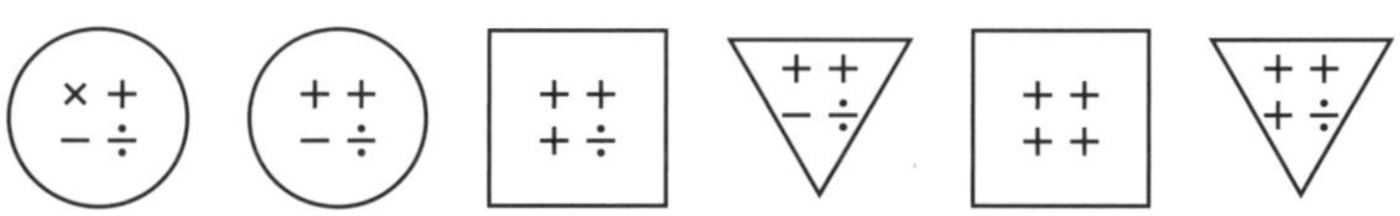

AX BX CZ BY DZ ?

DY CY BZ CX AY
a b c d e

11

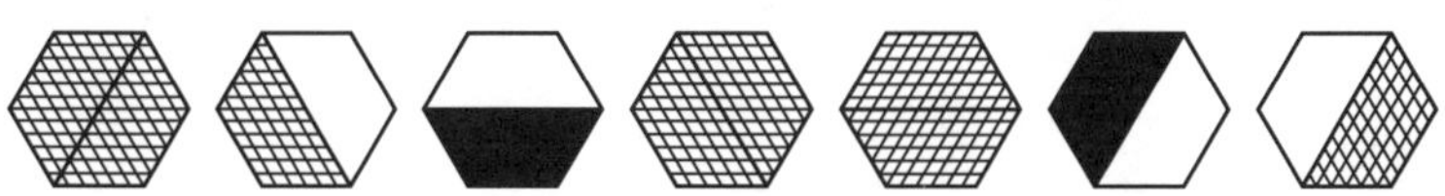

AT BU CS BT CT AS ?

BR AT CU BS AU
a b c d e

12

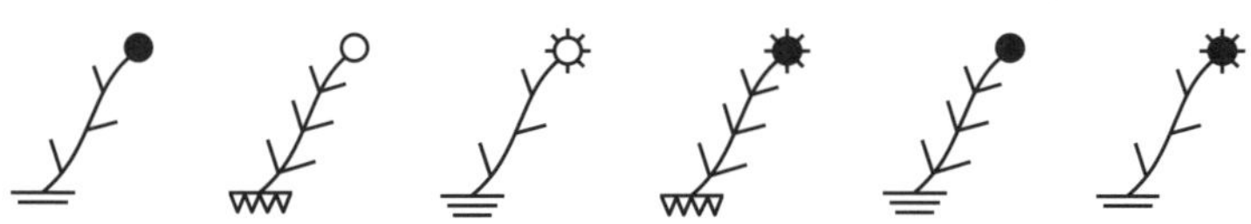

AX BZ DY CZ AY ?

AZ BZ CX DX CY
a b c d e

Total

TEST 2: Codes and Analogies

Test time: 0 5 10 minutes

Using the given patterns and codes, select the code that matches the last pattern.

Example

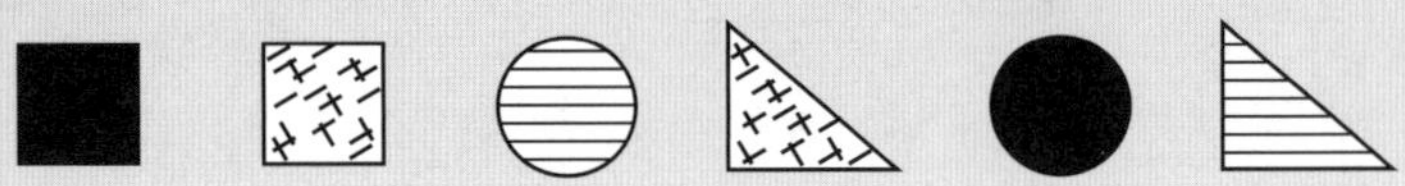

AX AY BZ CY BX ?

AY	AX	CZ	BZ	BY
a	b	(c)	d	e

1

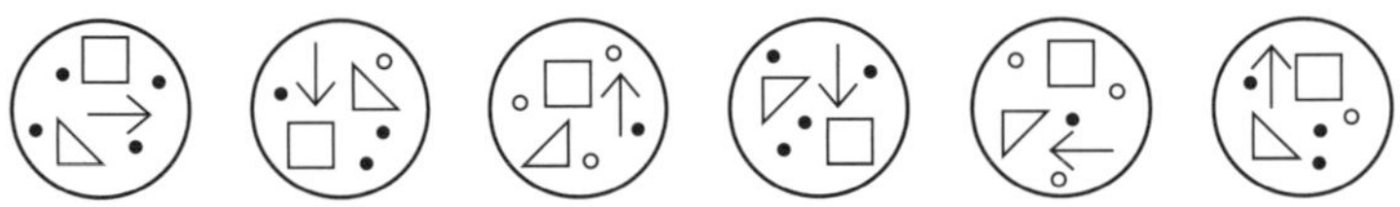

BX CY AZ CX DZ ?

AX	AY	CZ	DY	BZ
a	b	c	d	e

2

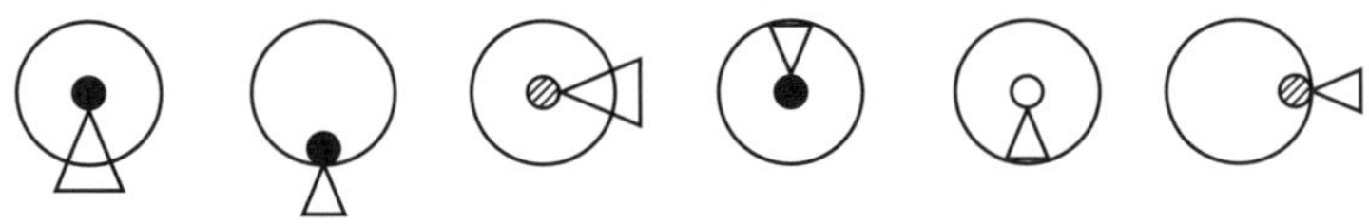

ER DR ES FR FT ?

ET	FS	DS	DT	ES
a	b	c	d	e

3

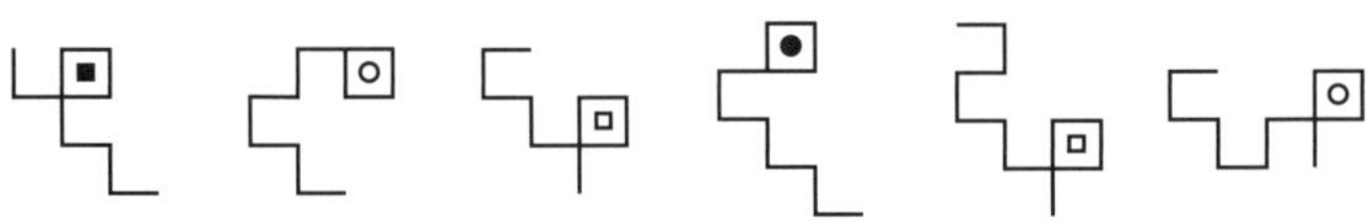

AH BJ AG BK CG ?

CH	BG	CJ	AK	BH
a	b	c	d	e

4

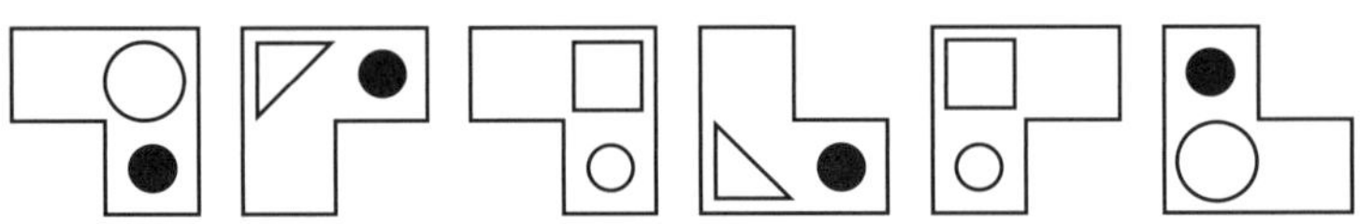

LX MY LZ NY MZ ?

LY	NZ	NX	MX	NY
a	b	c	d	e

5

AX BY CZ BZ DY ?

CX	CY	BZ	DZ	AY
a	b	c	d	e

6

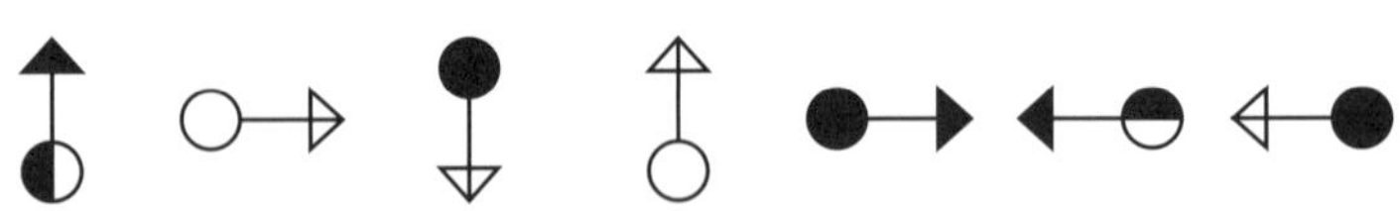

AY BX CZ AX BZ DY ?

AZ	BY	DX	DZ	CY
a	b	c	d	e

Which shape or pattern completes the second pair in the same way as the first pair?

Example

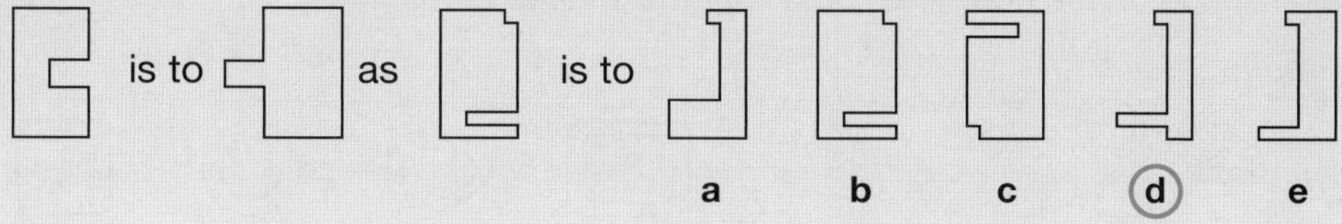

7

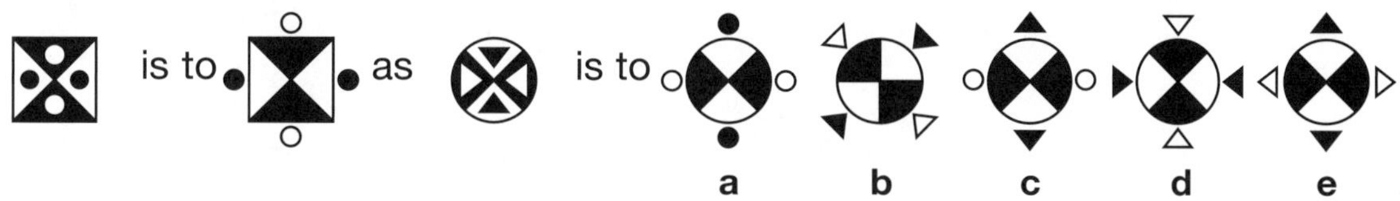

8

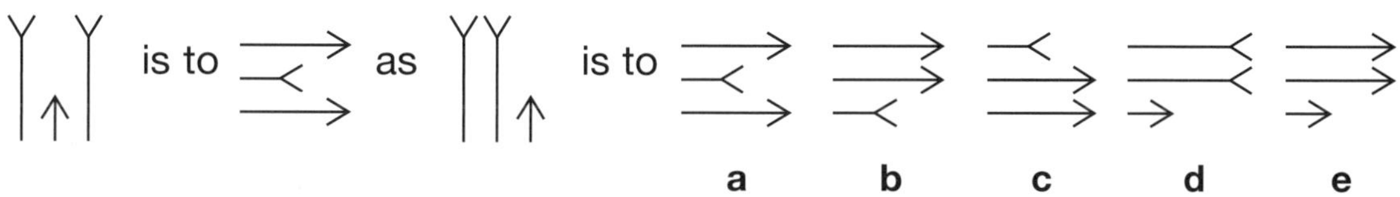

9

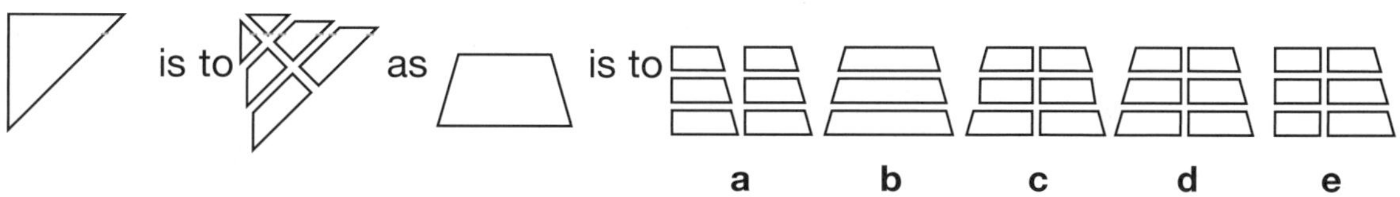

10

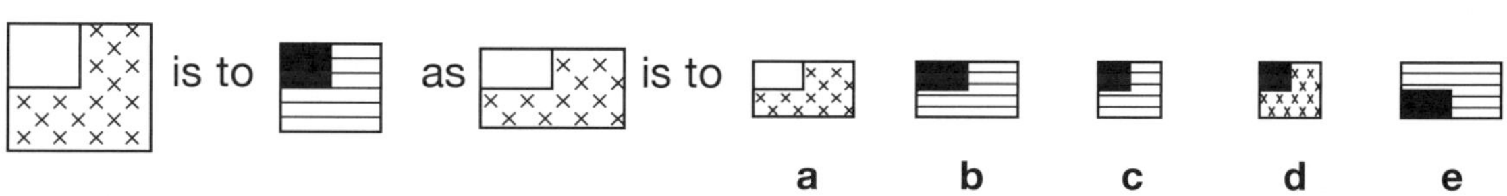

11

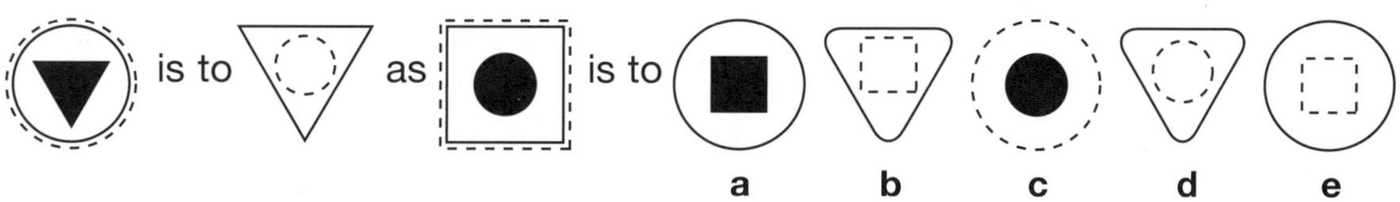

12

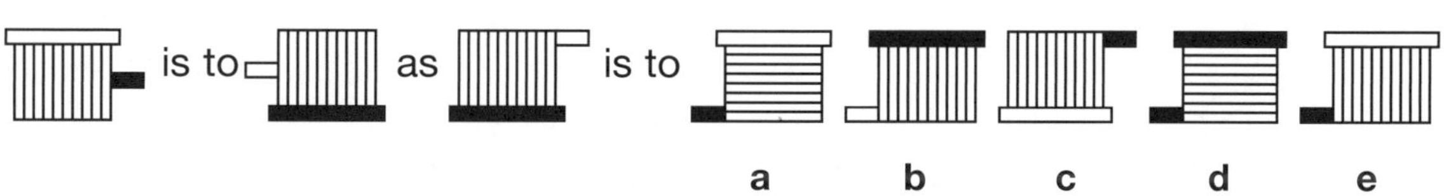

Total

TEST 3: Similarities and Sequences

Test time: 0 5 10 minutes

Which shape on the right goes best with the shapes on the left?

Example

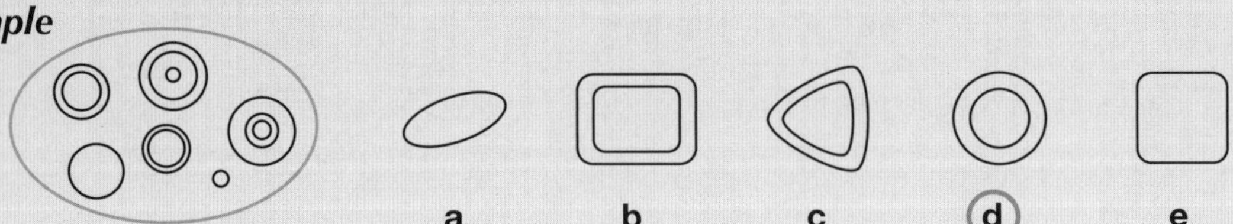

a b c d e

1 

a b c d e

2 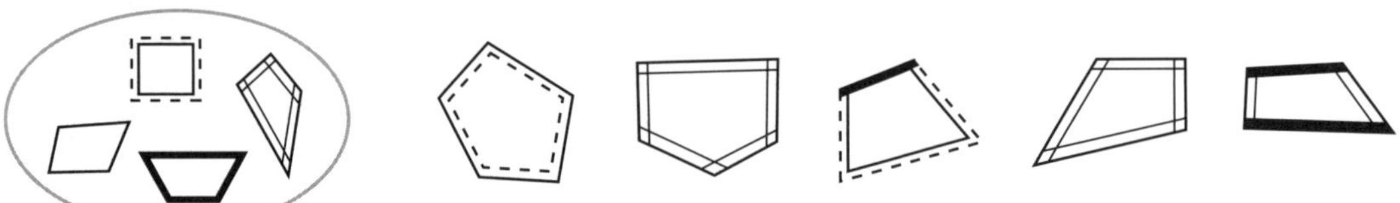

a b c d e

3 

a b c d e

4 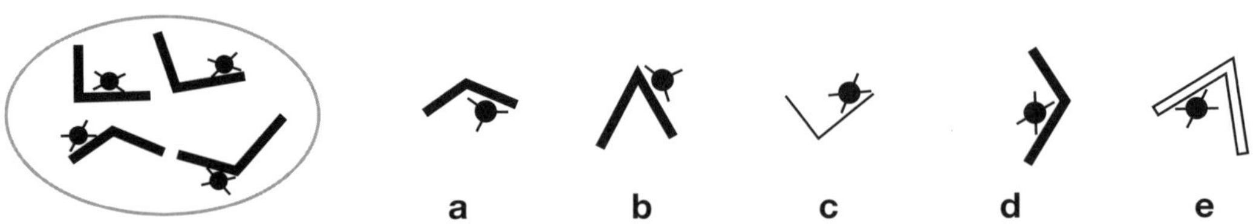

a b c d e

5 

a b c d e

6 

a b c d e

Which shape or pattern completes the larger grid?

Example

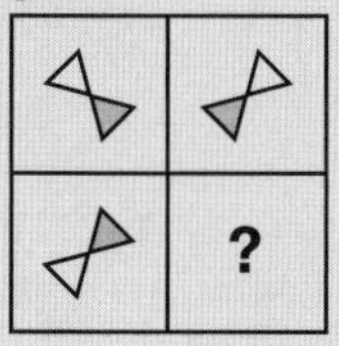

a b c (d) e

7

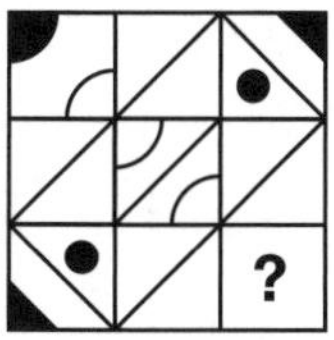

a b c d e

8

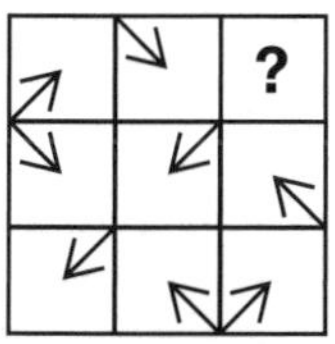

a b c d e

9

a b c d e

10

a b c d e

11

a b c d e

12

a b c d e

Total

Test 4: Sequences and Codes

Test time: 0 5 10 minutes

Which pattern continues or completes the given series?

Example

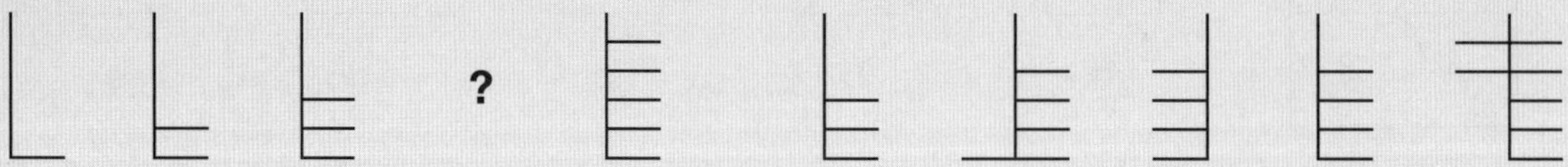

a b c (d) e

1

a b c d e

2

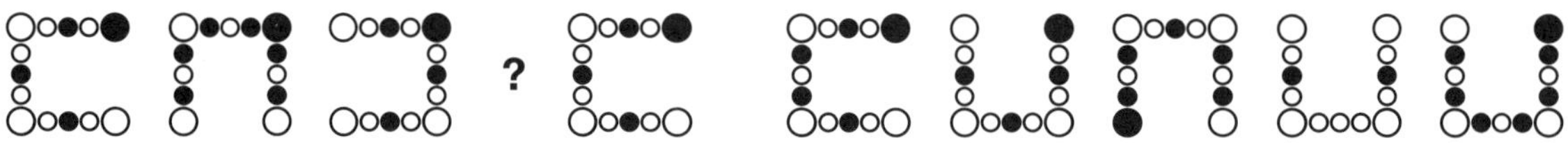

a b c d e

3

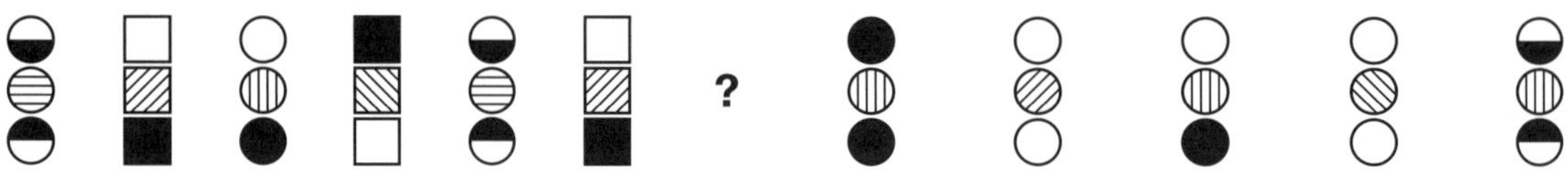

a b c d e

4

a b c d e

5

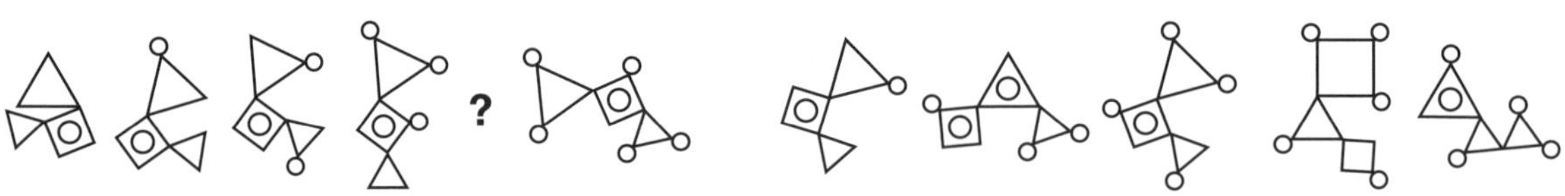

a b c d e

6

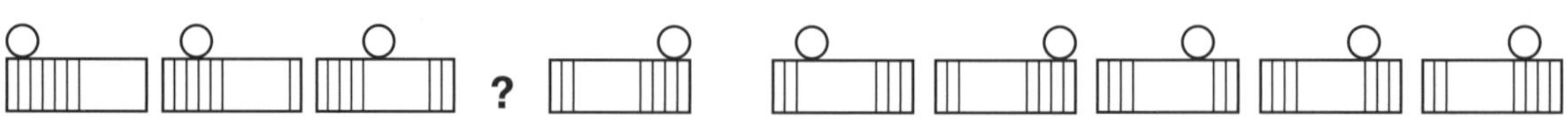

a b c d e

Using the given patterns and codes, select the code that matches the last pattern.

Example

AX AY BZ CY BX ?

AY AX CZ BZ BY
a b (c) d e

7

XP YR ZS XQ YP ?

ZR YS XS YQ ZQ
a b c d e

8

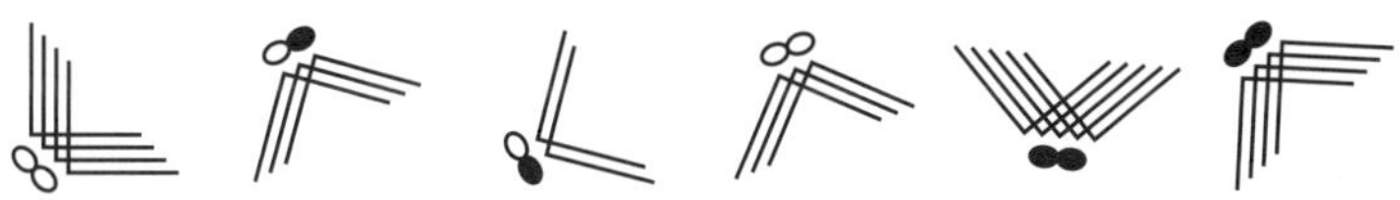

AN BM BL AM CO ?

CN BN CL AO AL
a b c d e

9

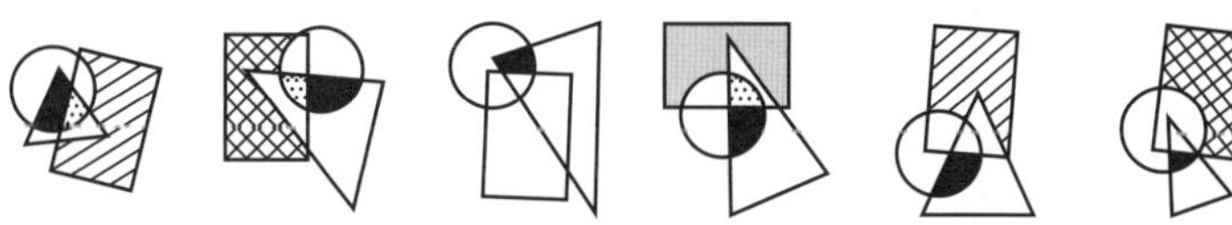

BX CX AY DX BY ?

DY CX CY AX DY
a b c d e

10

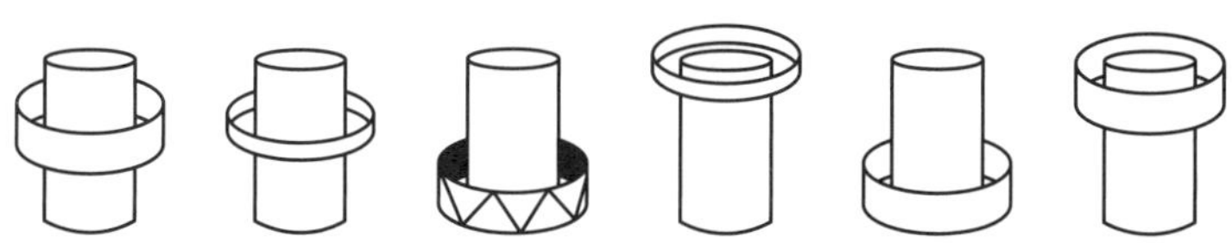

FM EM GL EN FL ?

EL FN GN GM FM
a b c d e

11

AX BY AZ CX BZ ?

AY BX CZ BY CY
a b c d e

12

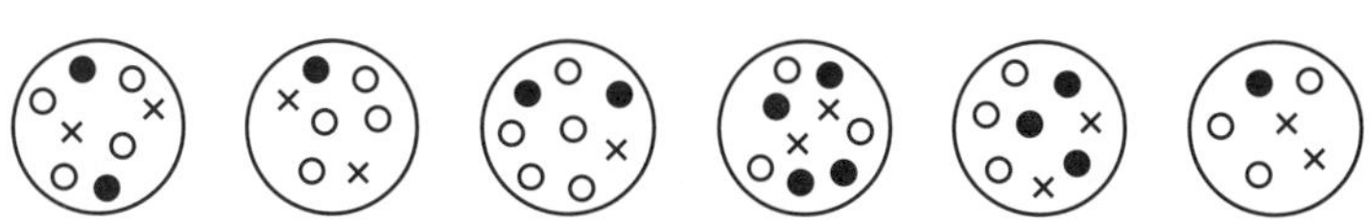

DX DW EX CZ CY ?

CW EW VX EY DZ
a b c d e

Time for a break! Go to Puzzle Page 42

Total

TEST 5: Cubes and Similarities

Test time: 0 5 10 minutes

Which cube could not be made from the given net?

Example

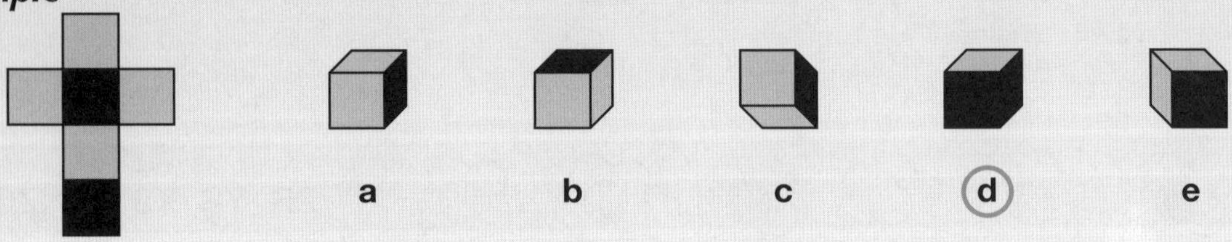

a b c (d) e

1

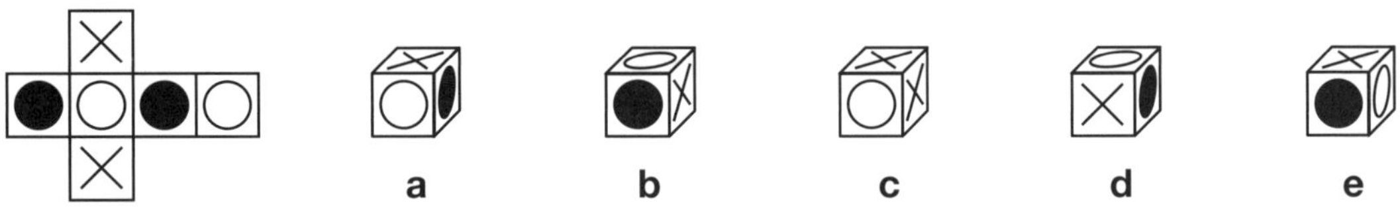

a b c d e

2

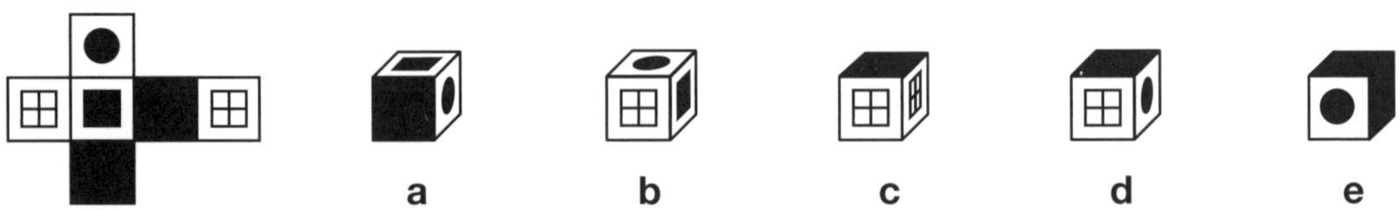

a b c d e

3

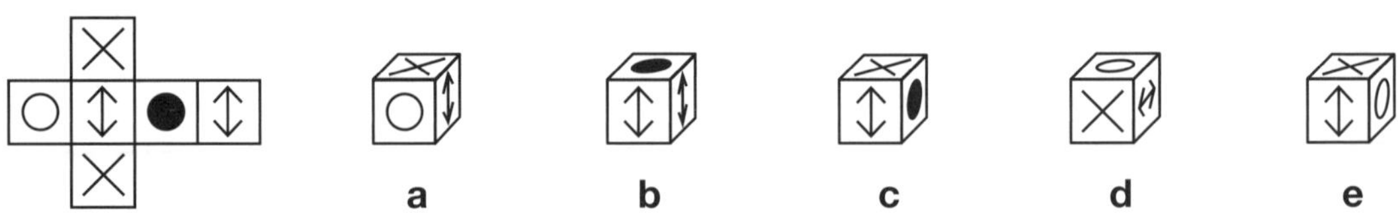

a b c d e

4

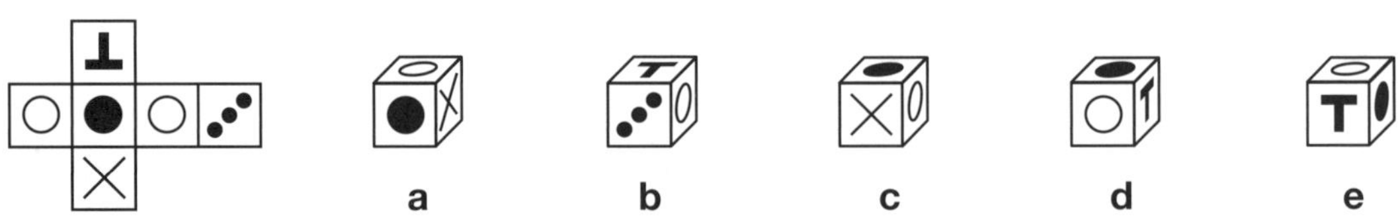

a b c d e

5

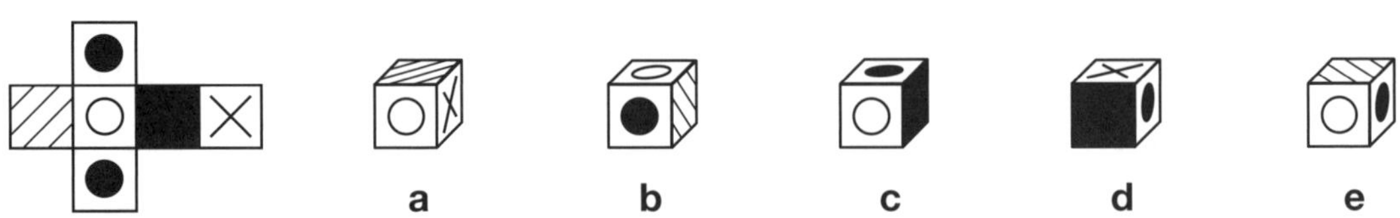

a b c d e

6

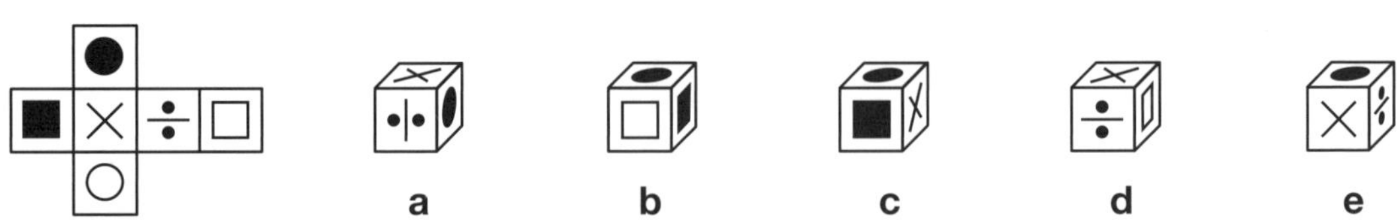

a b c d e

Which shape on the right goes best with the shapes on the left?

Example

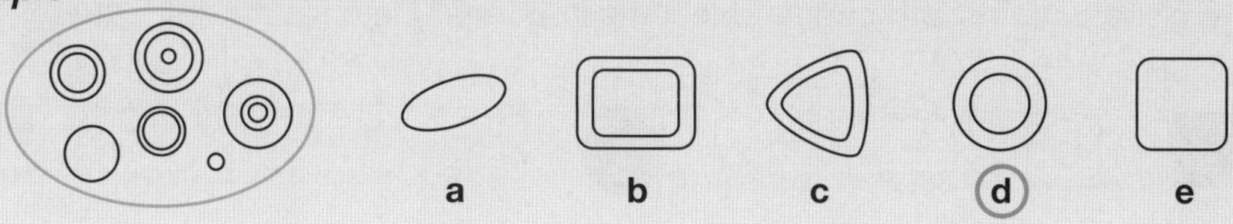

a b c d e

7

a b c d e

8

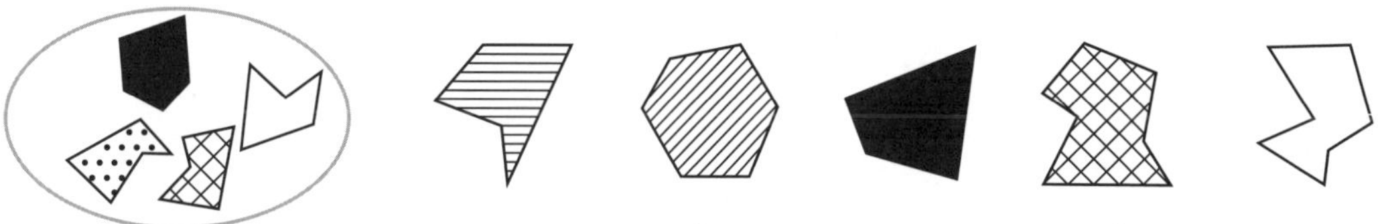

a b c d e

9

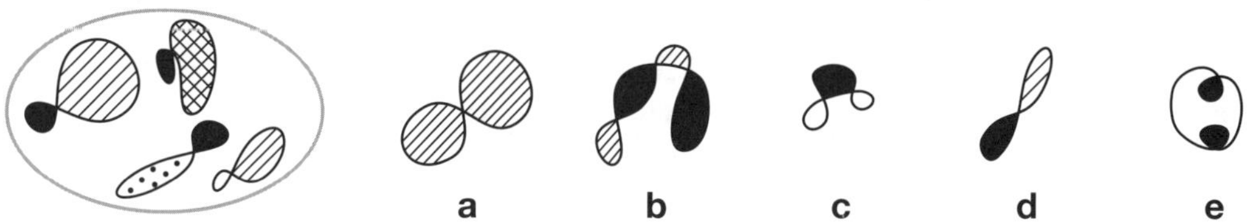

a b c d e

10

a b c d e

11

a b c d e

12

a b c d e

Total

Test 6: Codes and Analogies

Test time: 0 5 10 minutes

Using the given patterns and codes, select the code that matches the last pattern.

Example

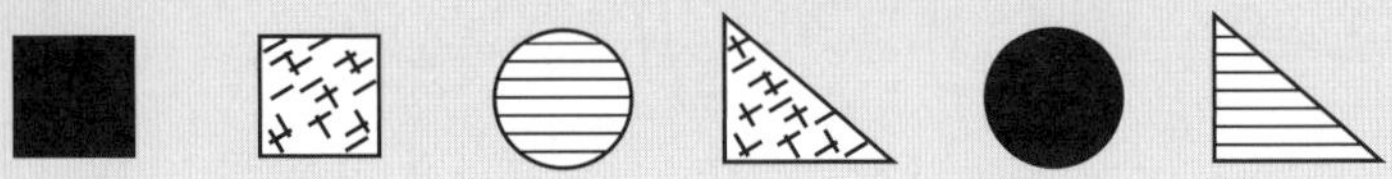

AX AY BZ CY BX ?

AY	AX	CZ	BZ	BY
a	b	(c)	d	e

1

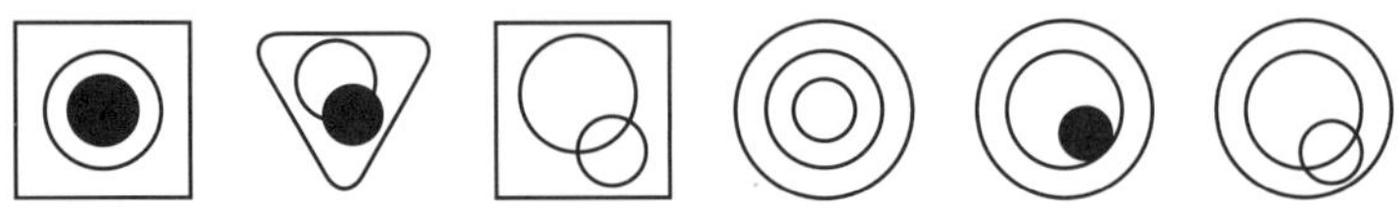

AZ BY CZ DX AX ?

CY	BX	CX	AY	DZ
a	b	c	d	e

2

BX AX CY BZ CX ?

CZ	BY	AZ	AY	BX
a	b	c	d	e

3

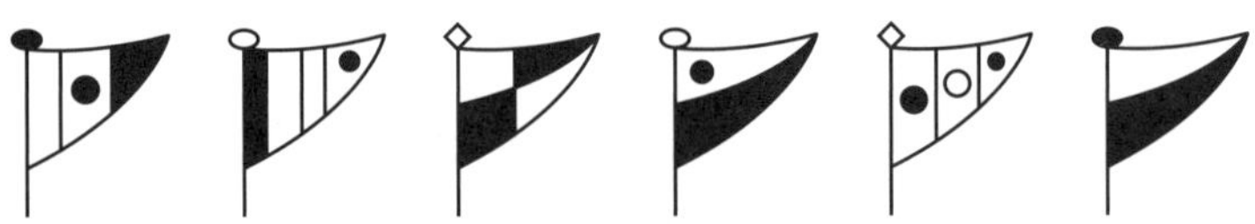

DM EN FN EL FM ?

DN	DL	EM	EL	FL
a	b	c	d	e

4

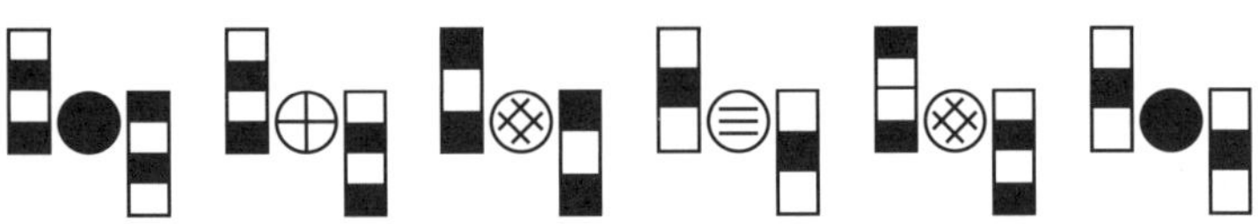

SE SF TG TH SG ?

TE	SH	TH	SE	TF
a	b	c	d	e

5

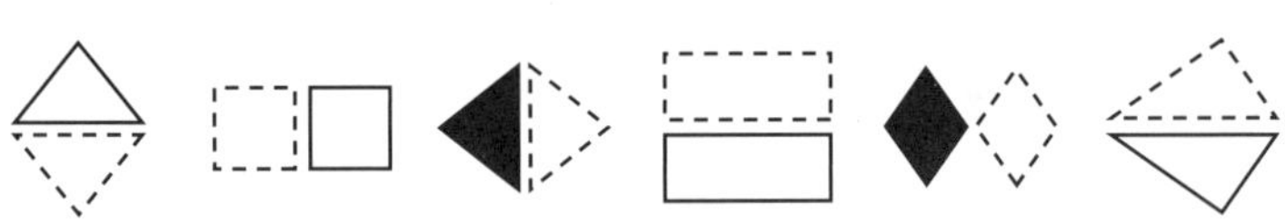

PS QW PE QN QE ?

QN	PW	PS	PN	QS
a	b	c	d	e

6

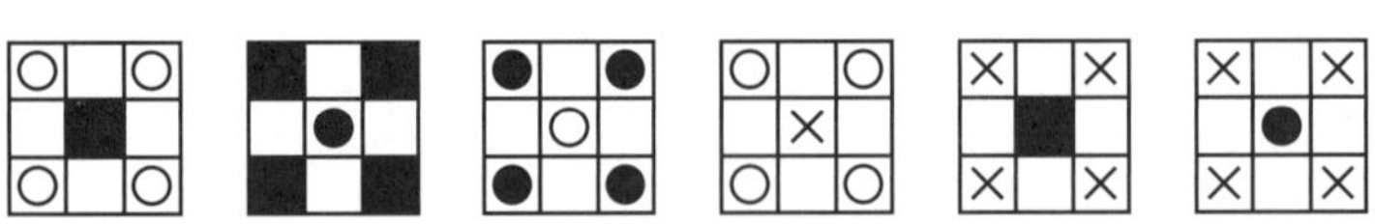

AG CF BE AH DG ?

CH	BF	DF	DH	AF
a	b	c	d	e

Which shape or pattern completes the second pair in the same way as the first pair?

Example

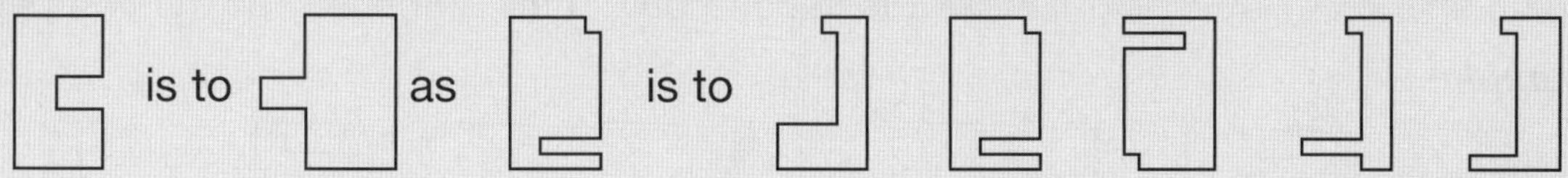

a b c (d) e

7

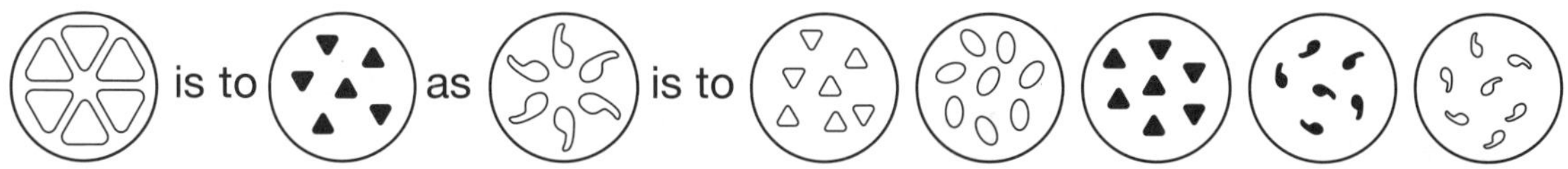

a b c d e

8

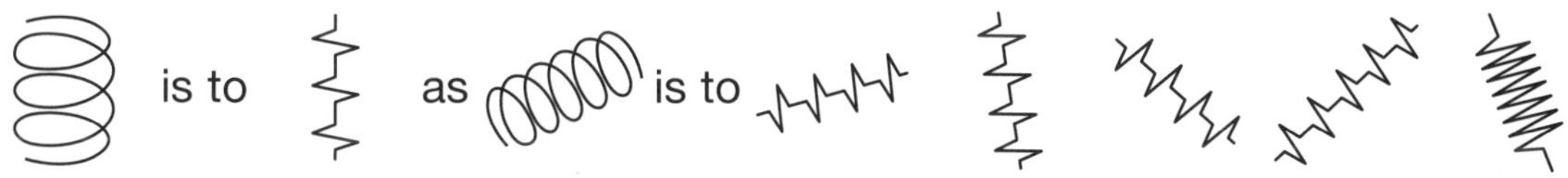

a b c d e

9

a b c d e

10

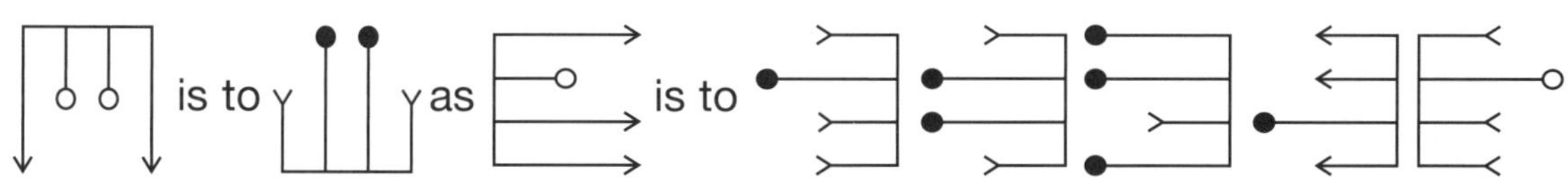

a b c d e

11

a b c d e

12

a b c d e

Total

TEST 7: Analogies and Cubes

Test time: 0 5 10 minutes

Which shape or pattern completes the second pair in the same way as the first pair?

Example

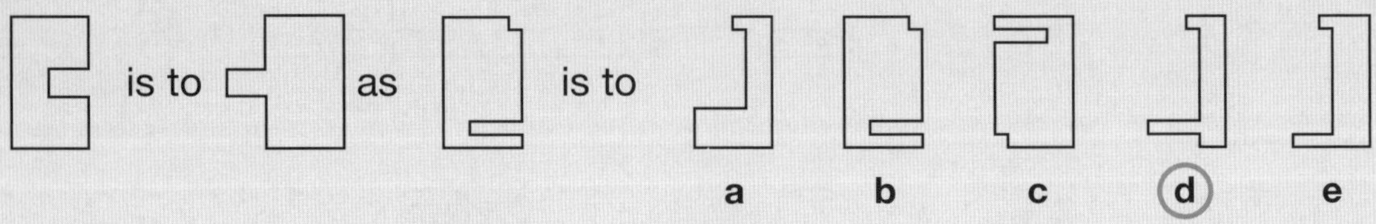

1

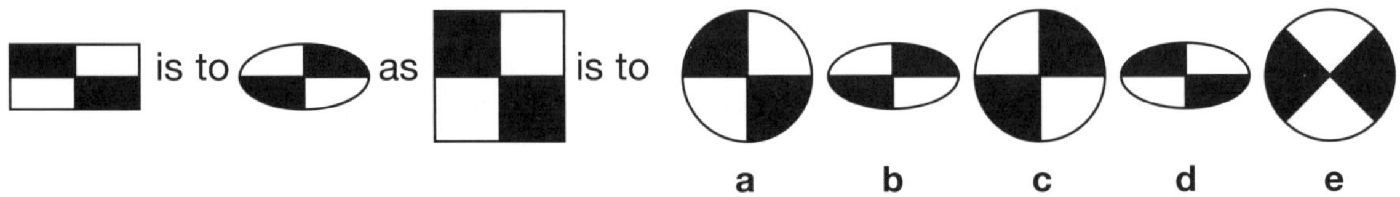

2

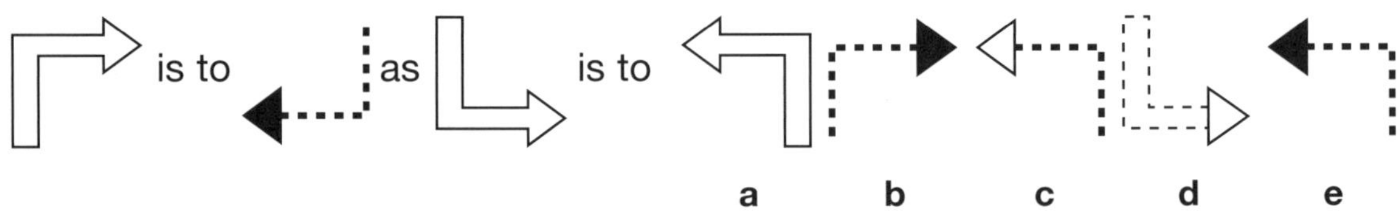

3

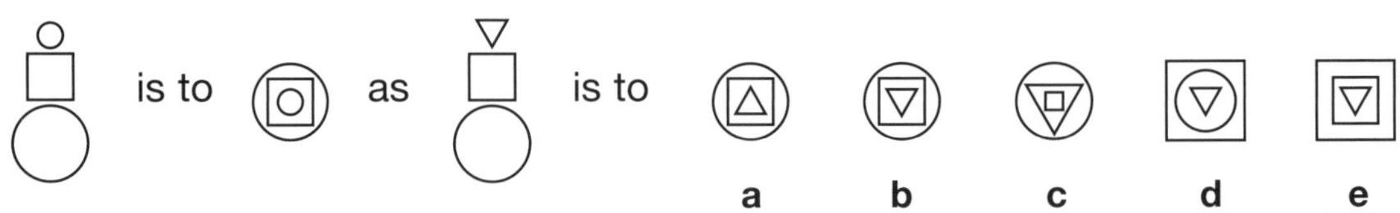

4

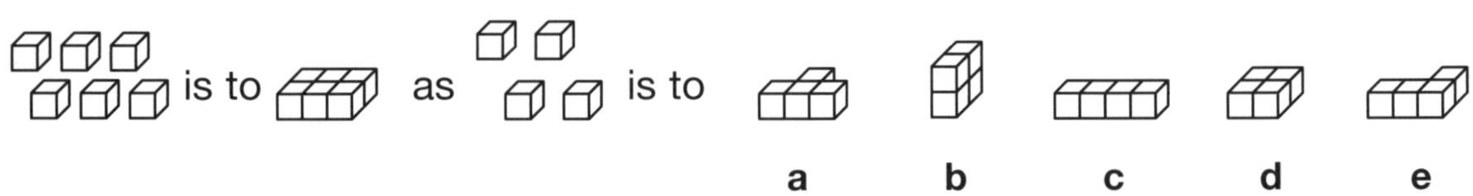

5

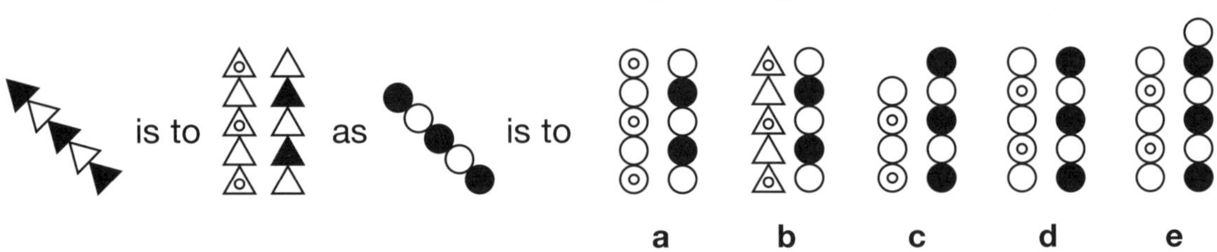

6

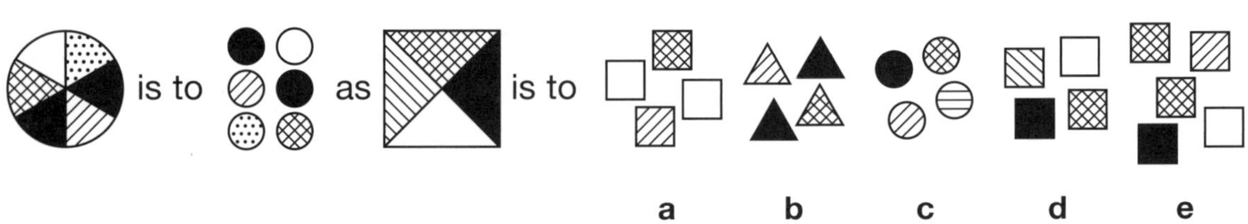

Which cube could not be made from the given net?

Example

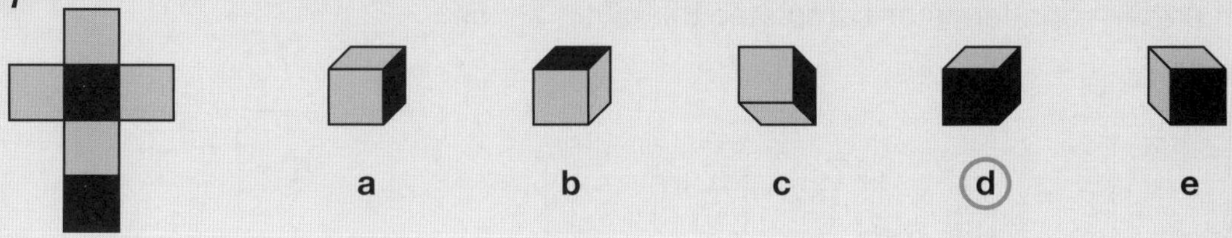

a b c (d) e

7

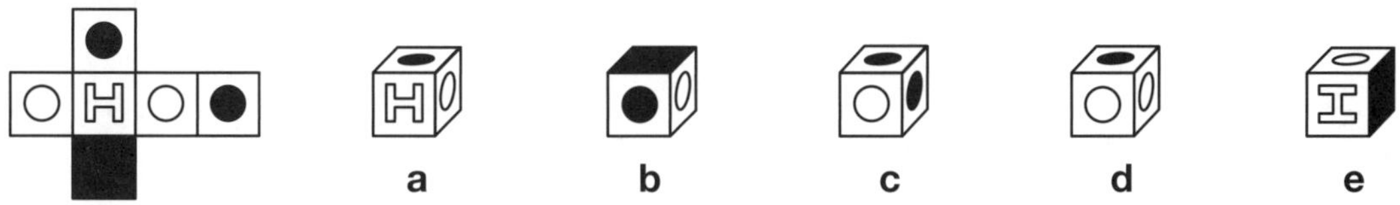

a b c d e

8

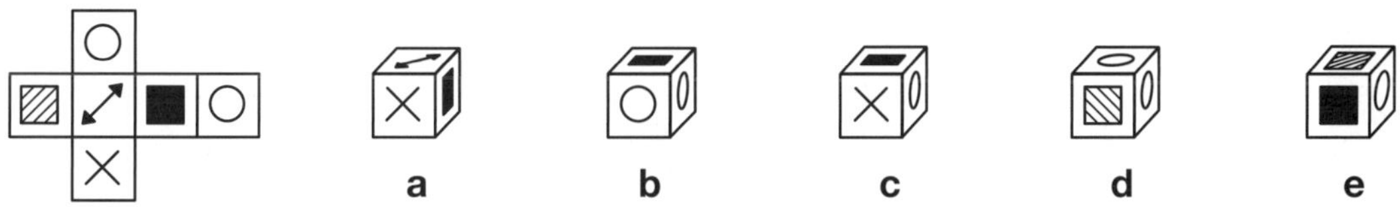

a b c d e

9

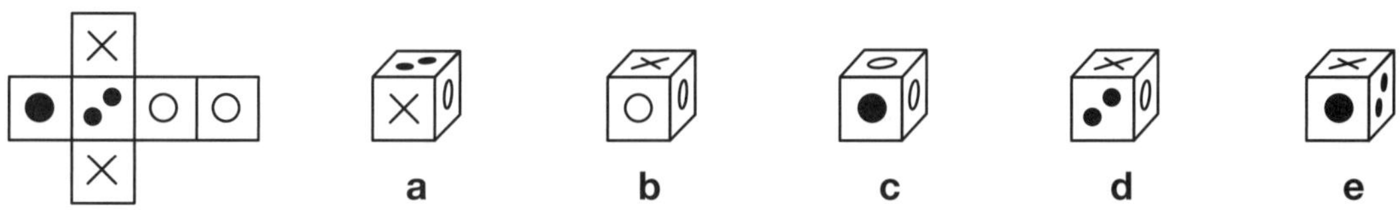

a b c d e

10

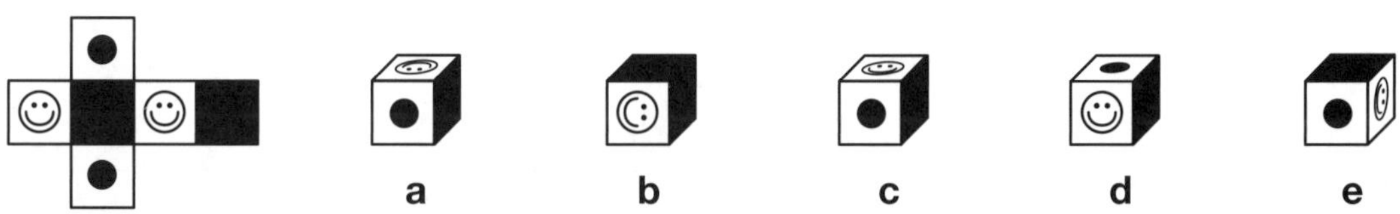

a b c d e

11

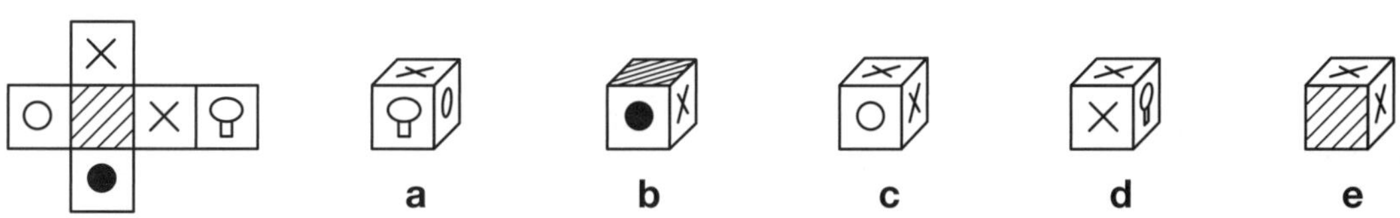

a b c d e

12

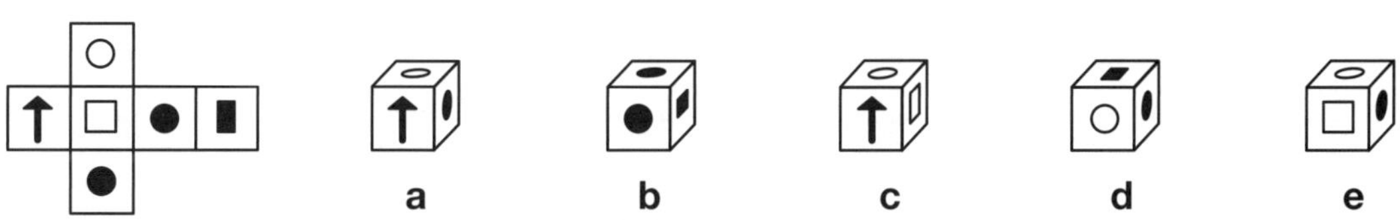

a b c d e

Total

Test 8: Sequences and Similarities

Test time: 0 5 10 minutes

Which pattern continues or completes the given series?

Example

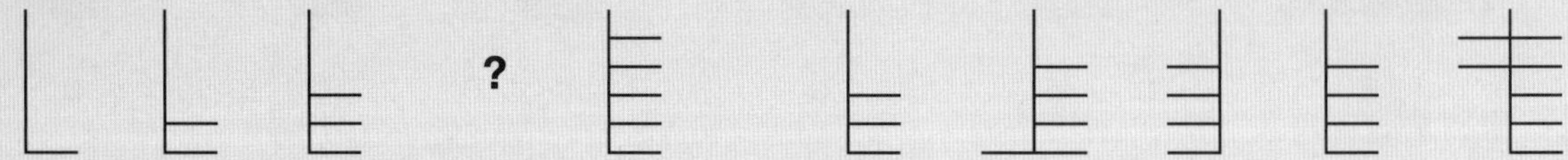

a b c d e

1

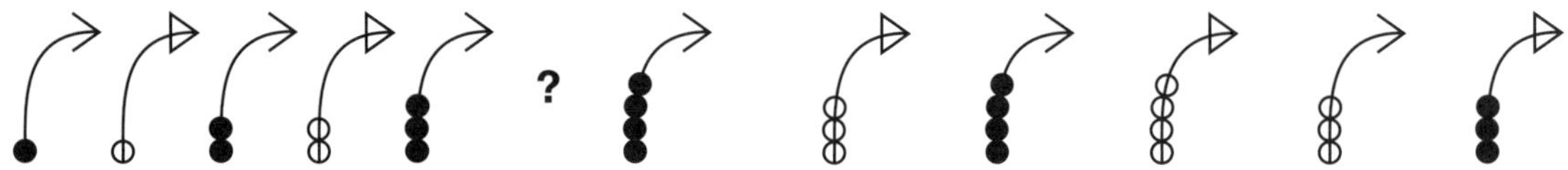

a b c d e

2

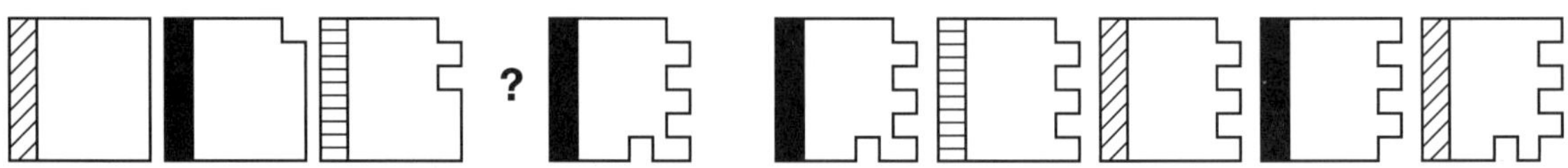

a b c d e

3

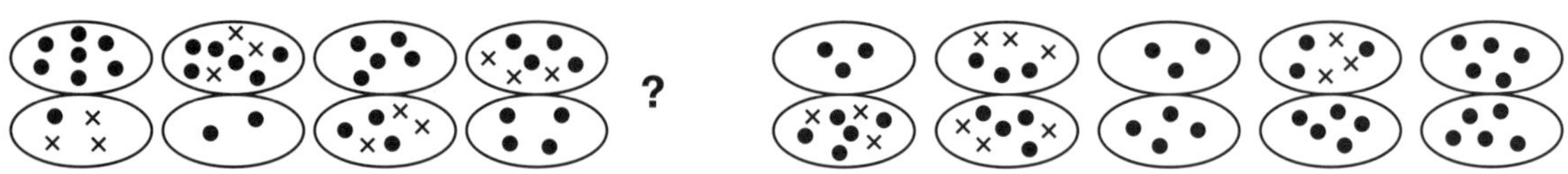

a b c d e

4

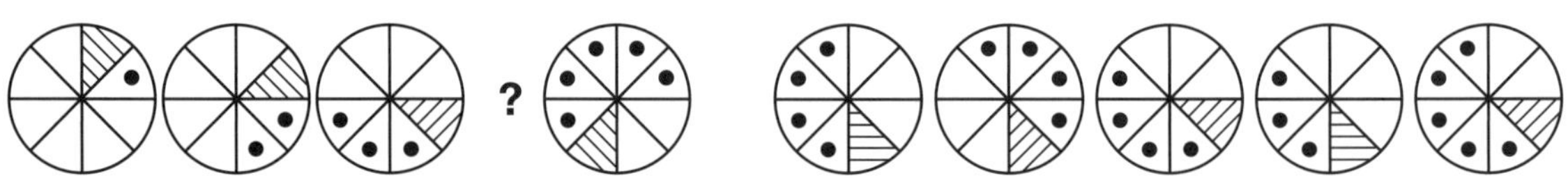

a b c d e

5

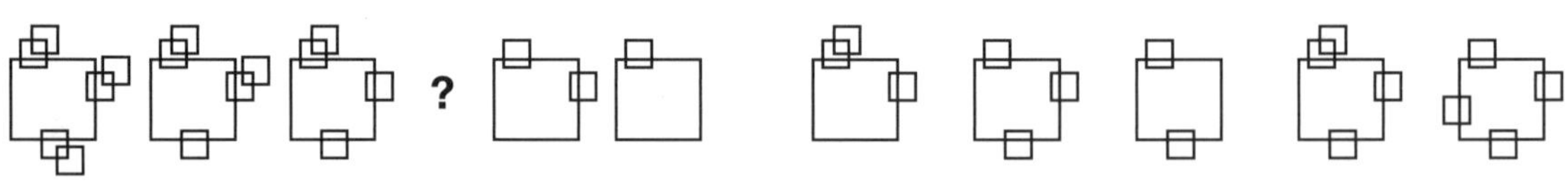

a b c d e

6

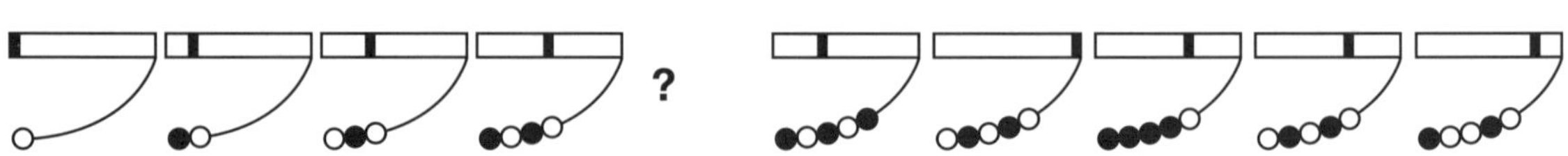

a b c d e

Which shape on the right goes best with the shapes on the left?

Example

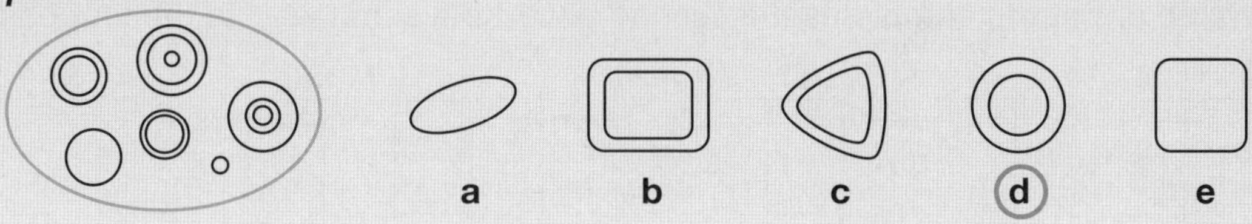

a b c d e

(d circled)

7

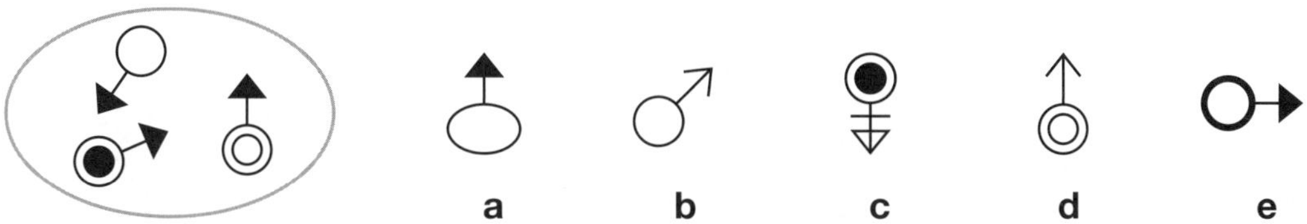

a b c d e

8

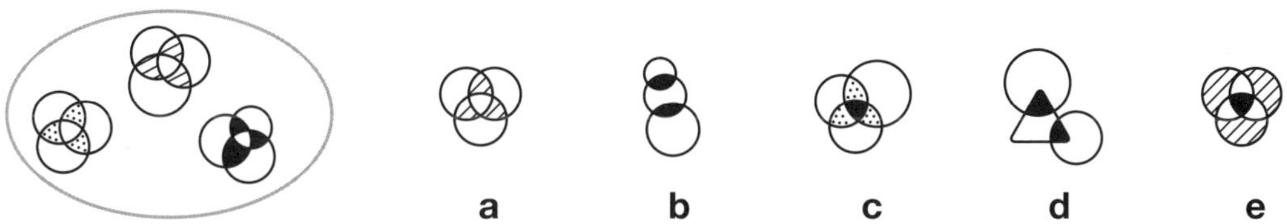

a b c d e

9

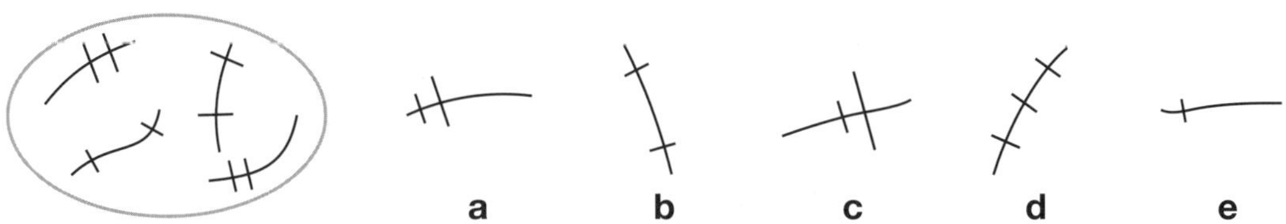

a b c d e

10

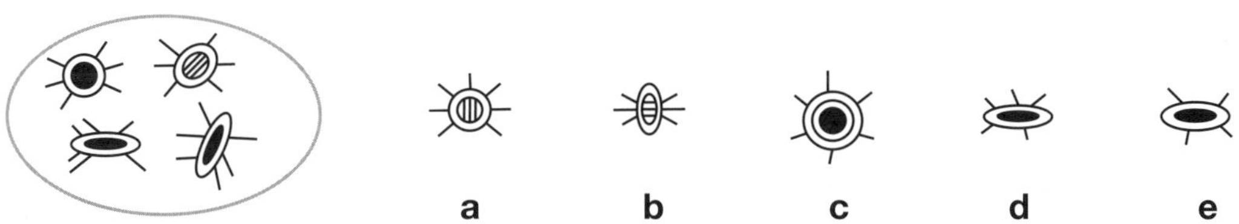

a b c d e

11

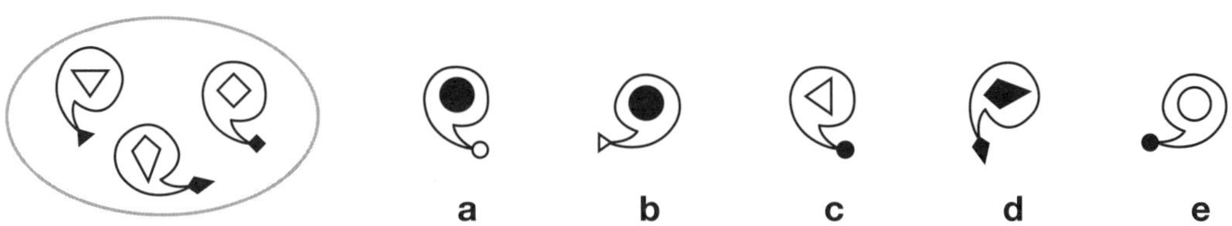

a b c d e

12

a b c d e

Time for a break! Go to Puzzle Page 43

Total

Test 9: Analogies and Similarities

Test time: 0 5 10 minutes

Which shape or pattern completes the second pair in the same way as the first pair?

Example

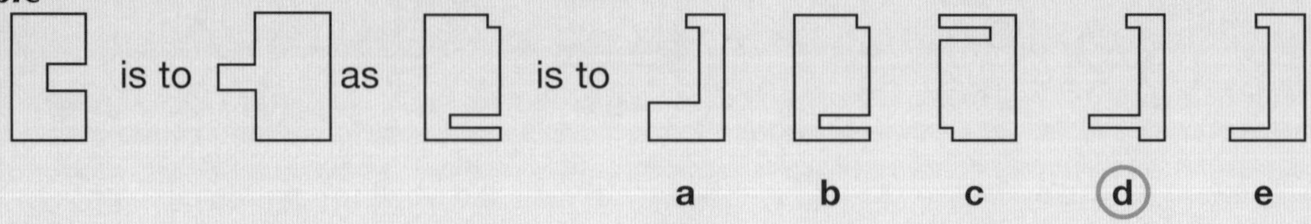

1

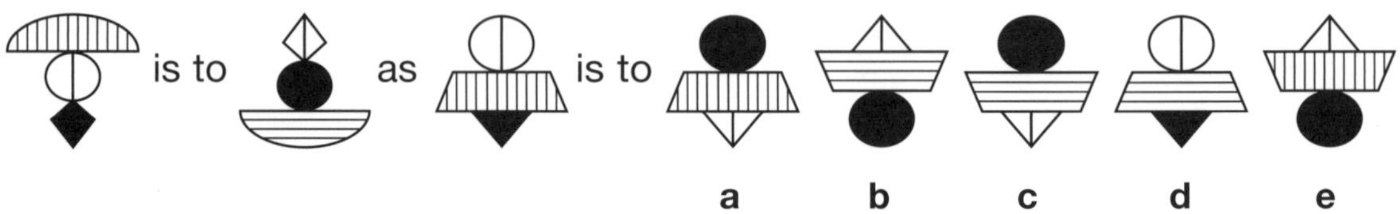

2

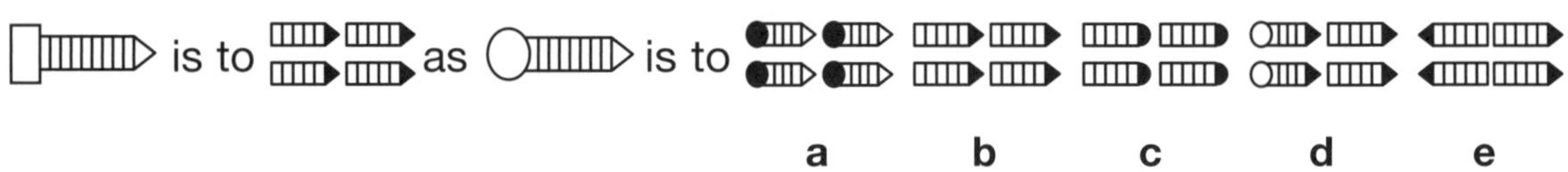

3

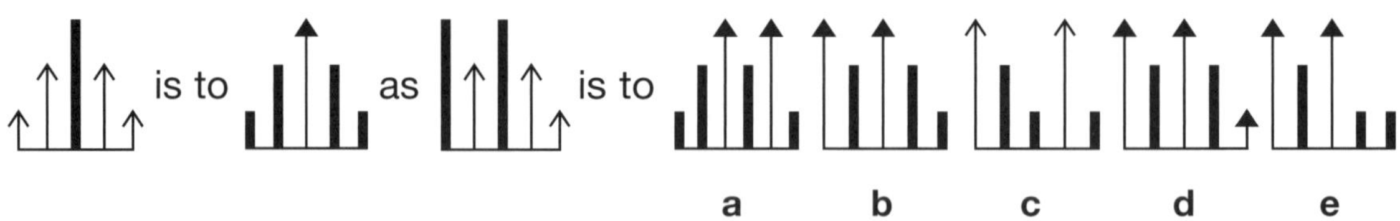

4

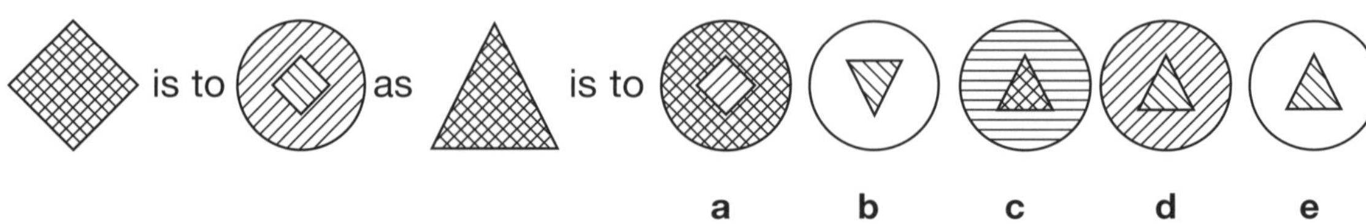

5

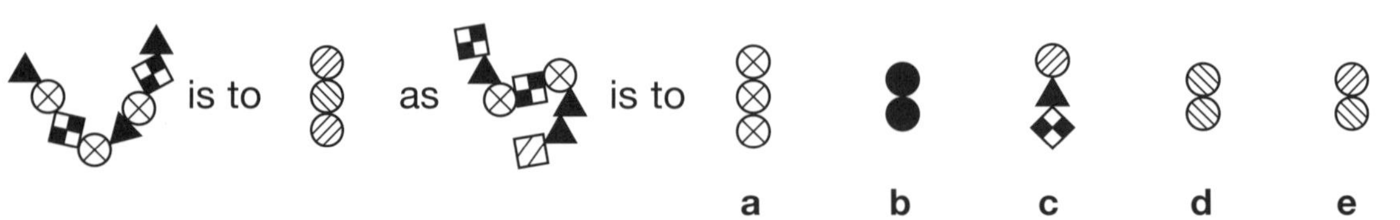

6

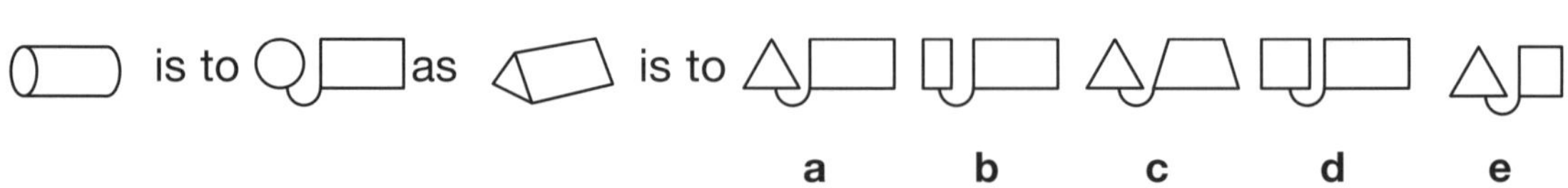

Which shape on the right goes best with the shapes on the left?

Example

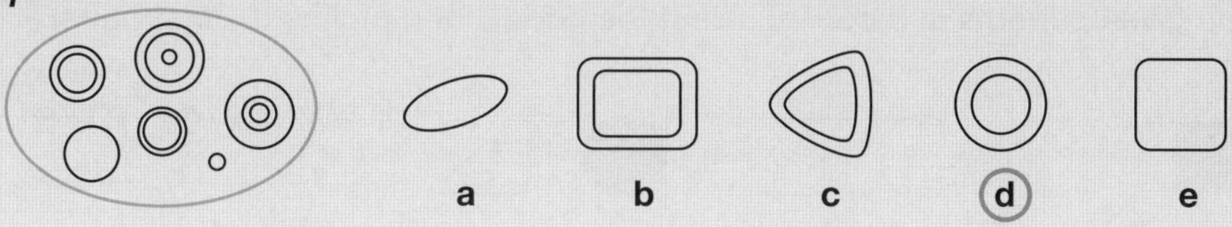

7

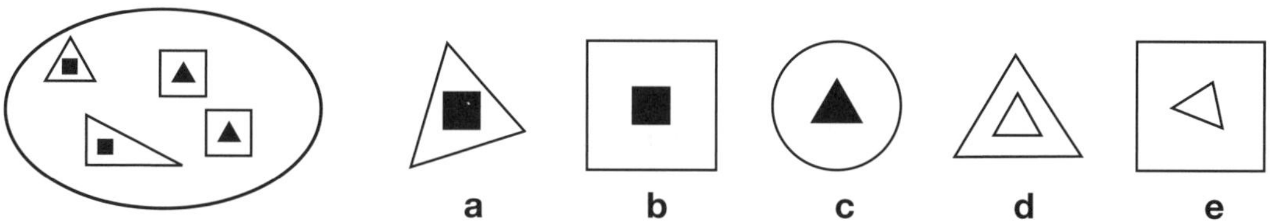

8

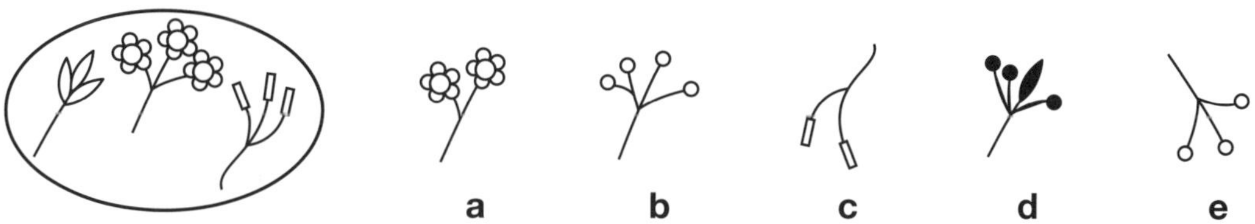

9

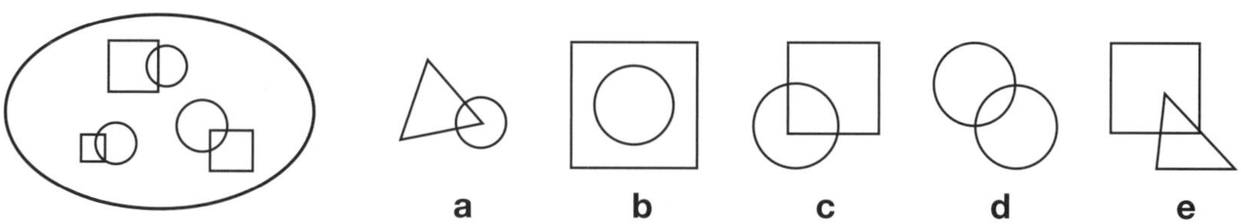

10

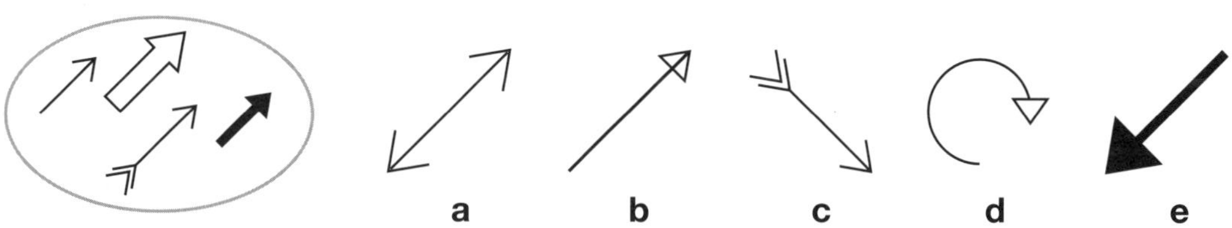

11

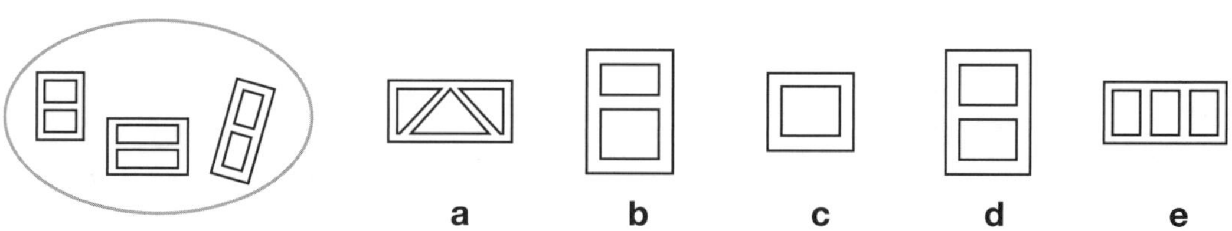

12

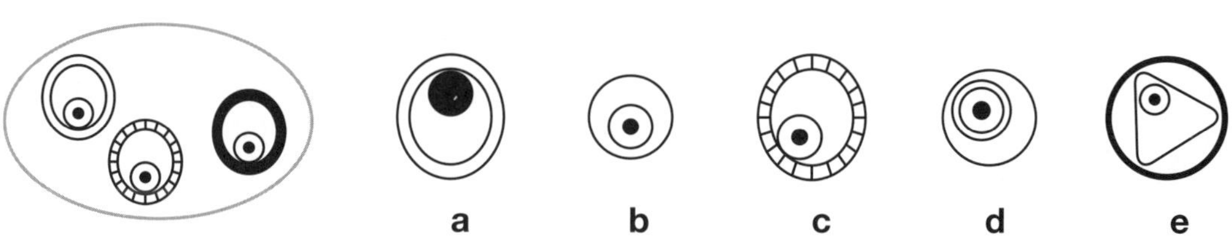

Total

Test 10: Codes and Cubes

Test time: 0 5 10 minutes

Using the given patterns and codes, select the code that matches the last pattern.

Example

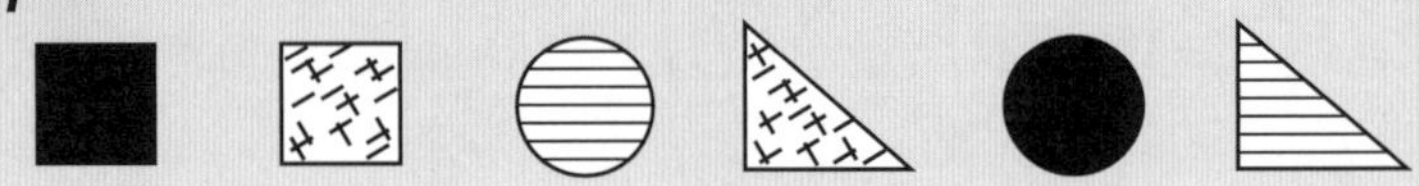

AX AY BZ CY BX ?

AY AX CZ BZ BY
a b (c) d e

1

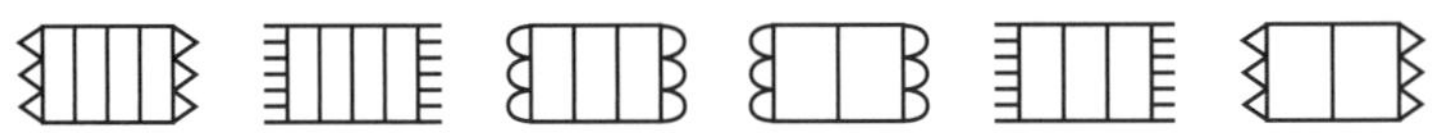

XL XM YN ZN YM ?

ZL XN XL ZM YL
a b c d e

2

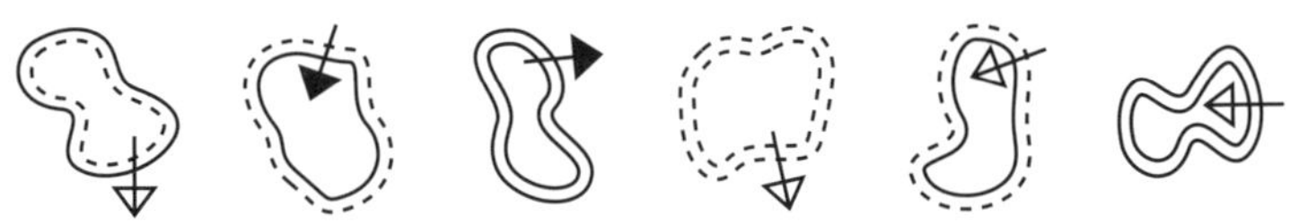

LD MG NF OD ME ?

OG LE NE MF ND
a b c d e

3

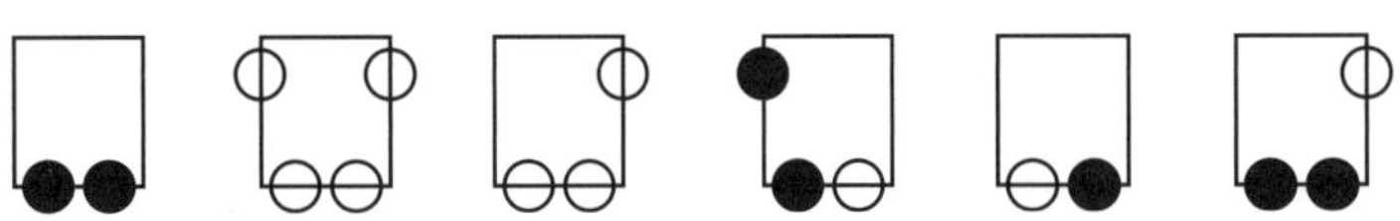

AT BV BU CU CT ?

AT AV CV BT CU
a b c d e

4

FA DB GA DC EB ?

EA DA GC GB FB
a b c d e

5

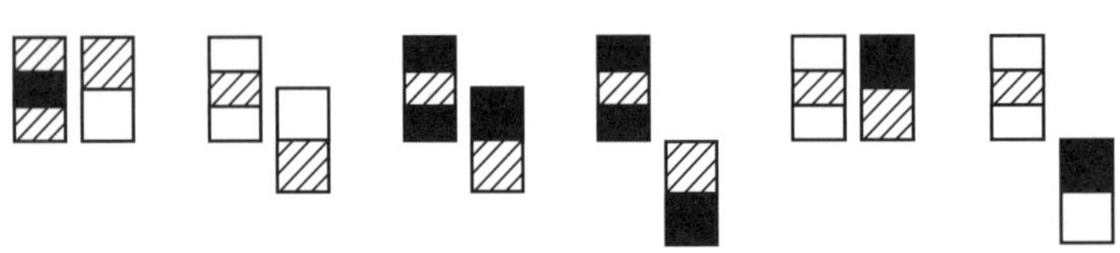

LX MY NY NZ MX ?

LY MX NX LX MZ
a b c d e

6

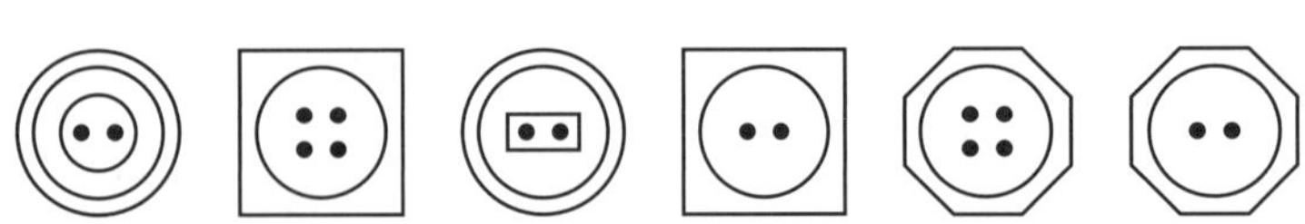

BF DG CF AG DH ?

AF DF CH AH BH
a b c d e

Which cube could not be made from the given net?

Example

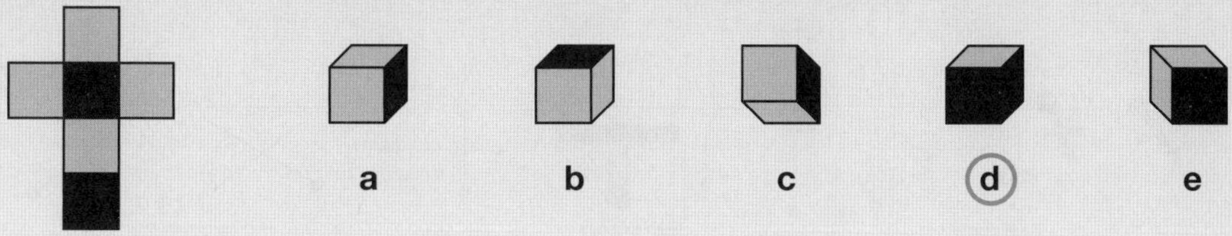

7

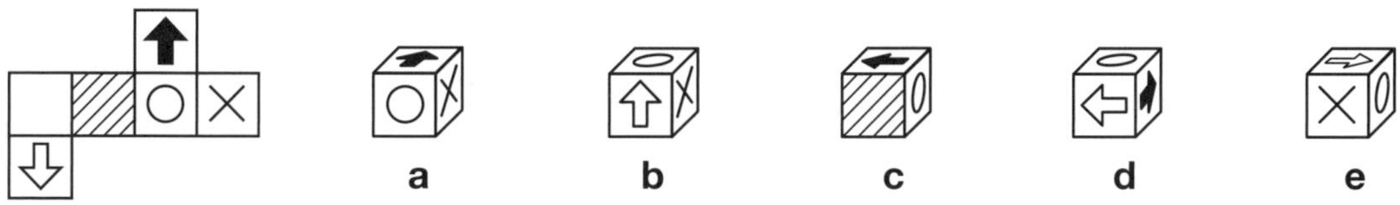

8

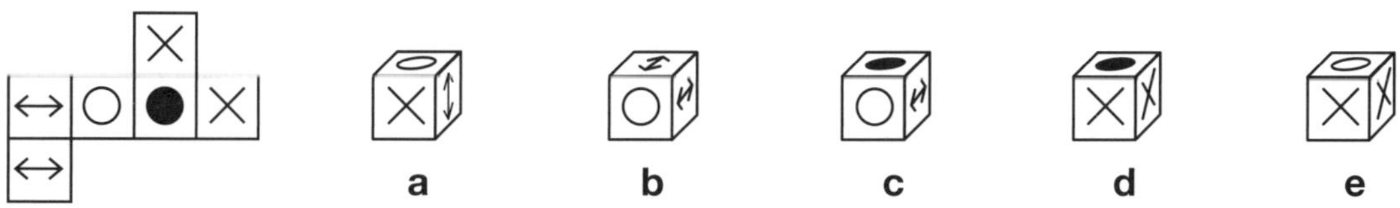

9

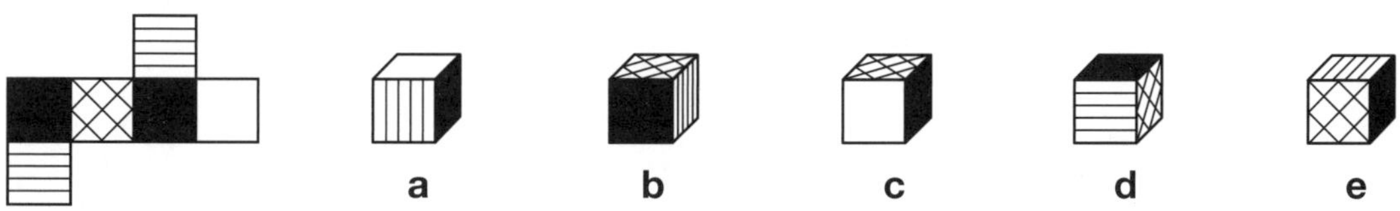

10

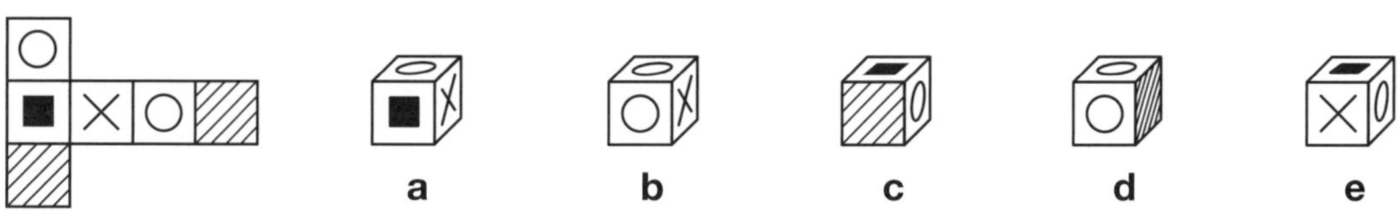

11

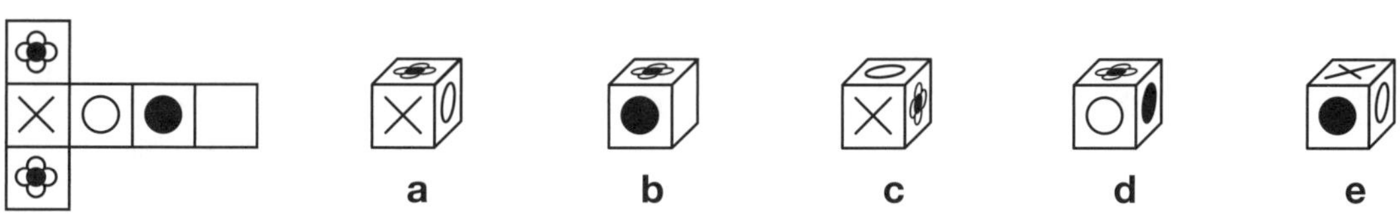

12

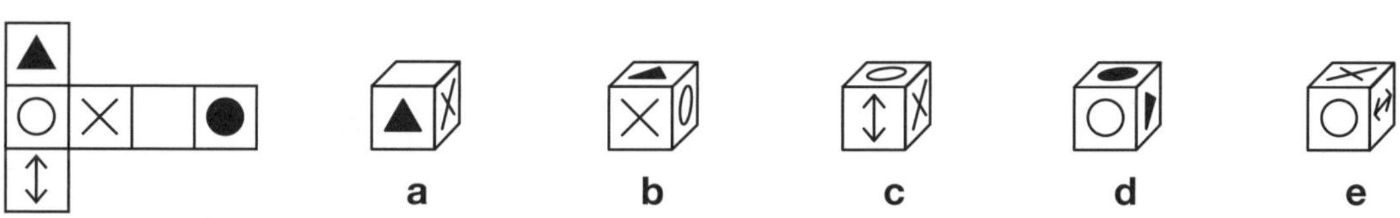

Total

Test 11: Mixed

Test time: 0 5 10 minutes

Which shape on the right goes best with the shapes on the left?

1
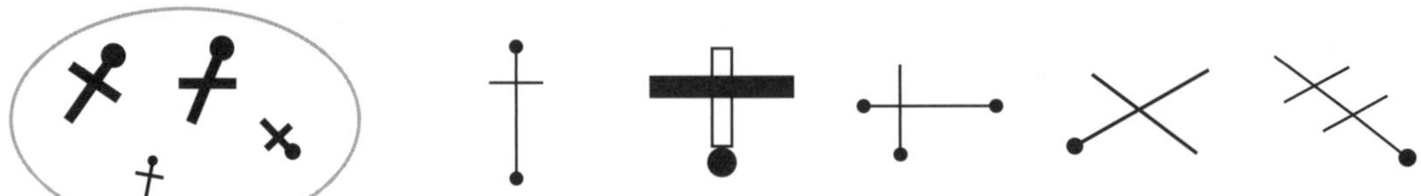
a b c d e

2
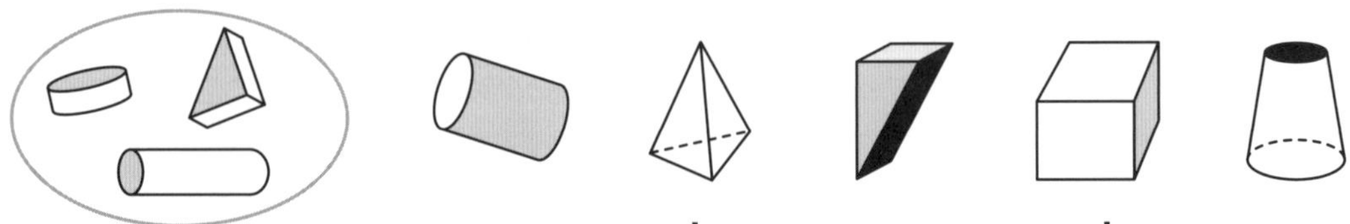
a b c d e

3
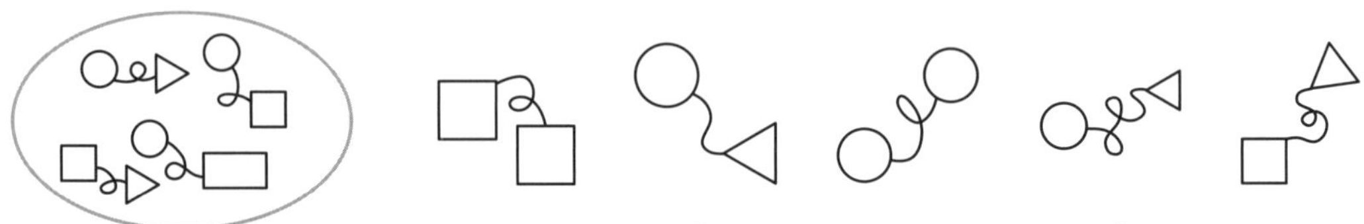
a b c d e

Which pattern continues or completes the given series?

4
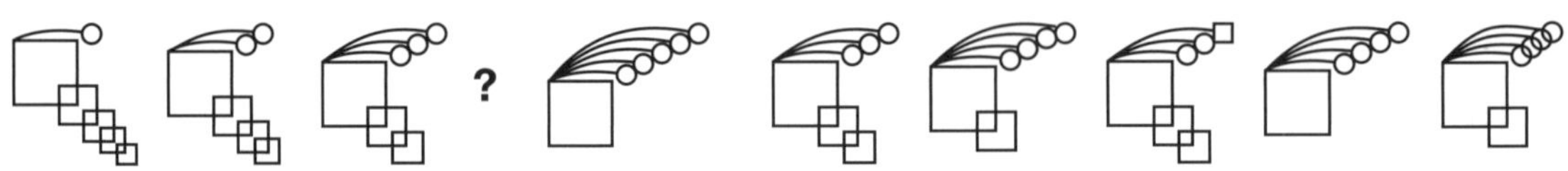
a b c d e

5
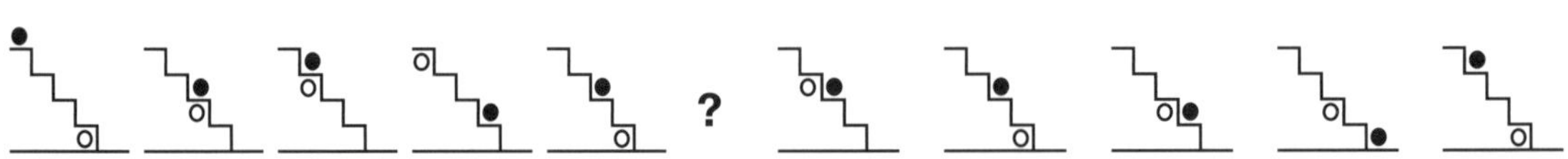
a b c d e

6
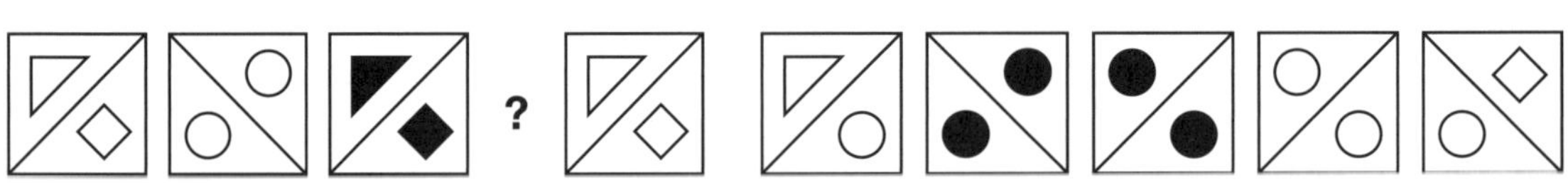
a b c d e

Which shape or pattern completes the second pair in the same way as the first pair?

7

a b c d e

8
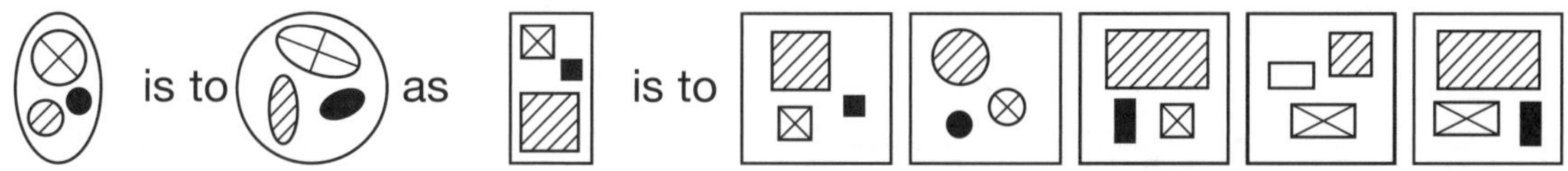

a b c d e

9
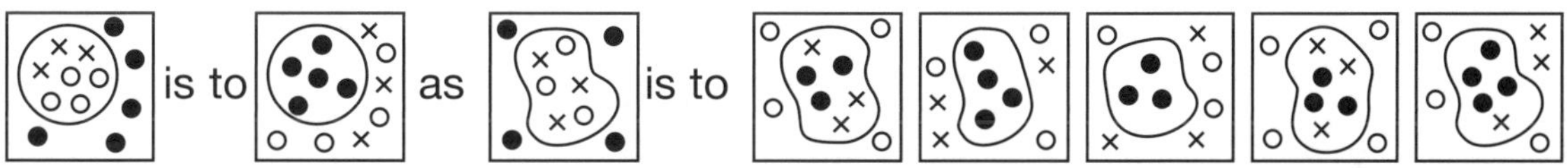

a b c d e

Using the given patterns and codes, select the code that matches the last pattern.

10
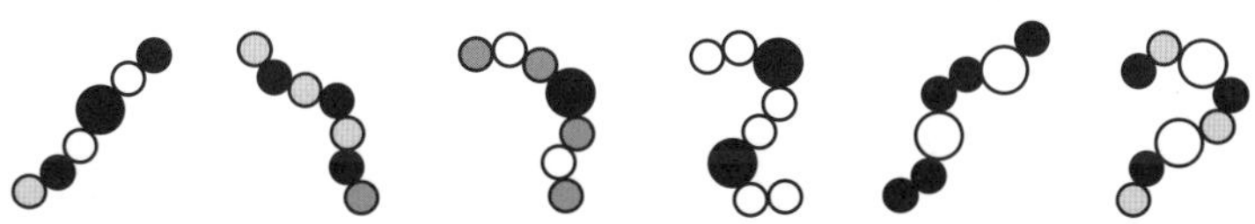

BX AZ BY DY CX ?

CY CZ DX AY BZ
a b c d e

11

AX CY BX DY BZ ?

AZ BZ DX CZ AY
a b c d e

12

LY MZ NZ OX MY ?

NY LX LZ NX OY
a b c d e

Total

Test 12: Mixed

Test time: 0 5 10 minutes

Which pattern continues or completes the given series?

1

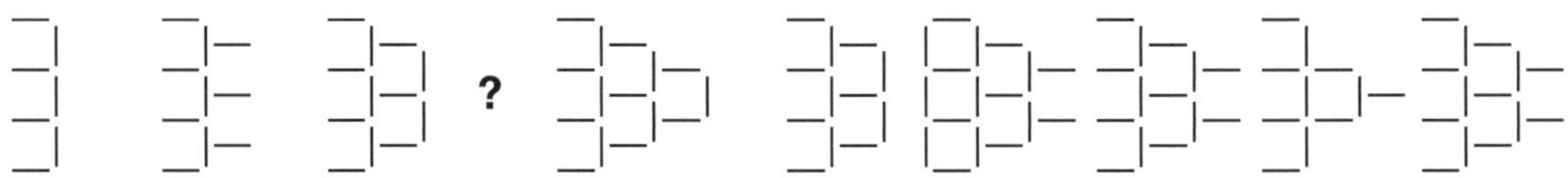

a b c d e

2

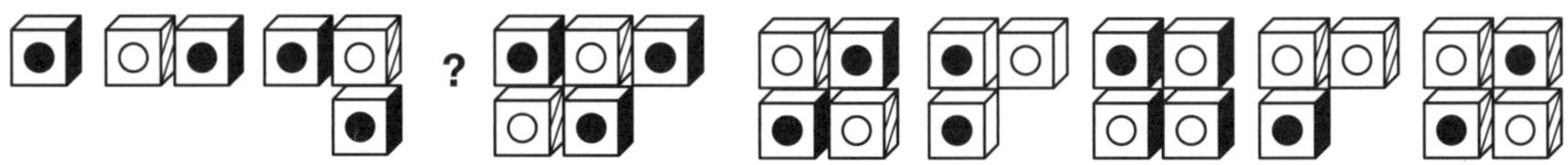

a b c d e

3

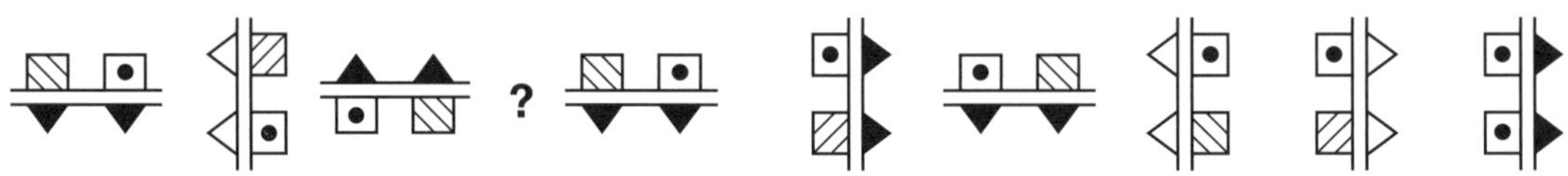

a b c d e

Which cube could not be made from the given net?

4

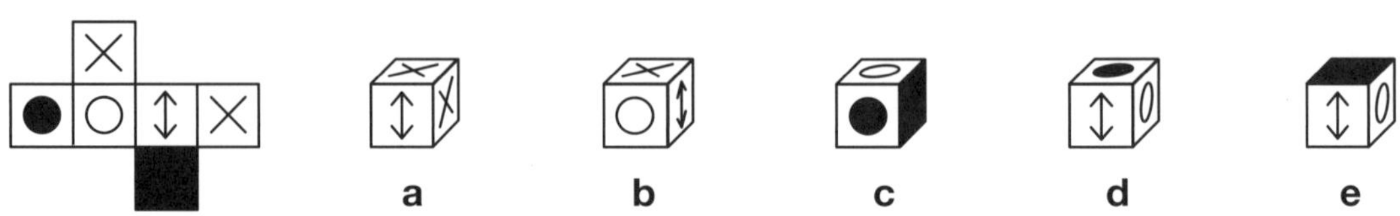

a b c d e

5

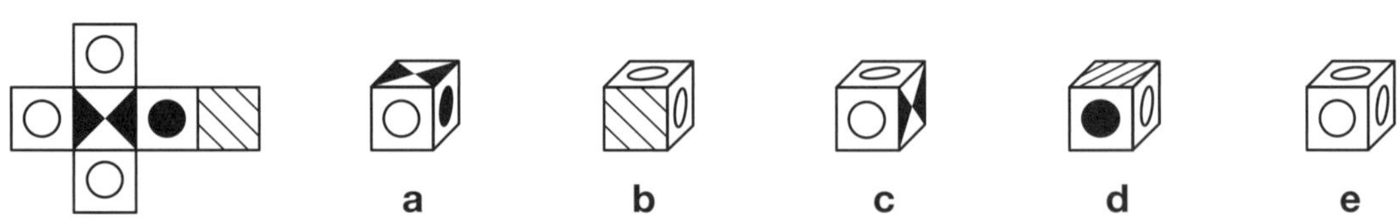

a b c d e

6

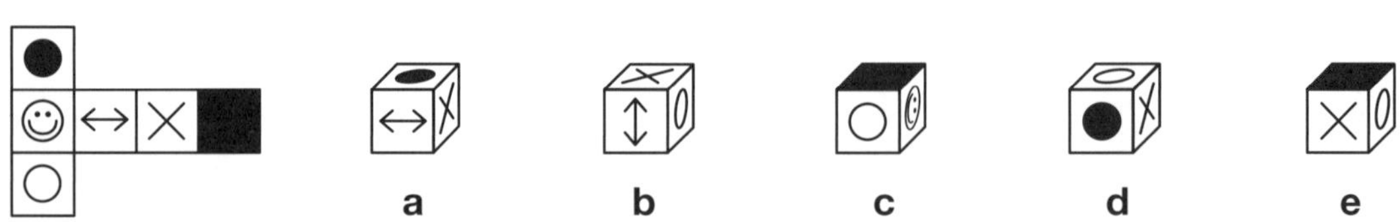

a b c d e

Test 1 (pages 2–3)

1 **b** The first and alternate shapes in the sequence are inverted Vs.
2 **e** The column of white circles alternates with the black circles and decreases by two each time.
3 **e** The shape is rotated clockwise by 90° and after a full turn the shape decreases by two lines, one at each end of the pattern.
4 **c** The pattern of black spots alternates with the crosses and increases by two each time.
5 **d** The vertical line reduces in height along the sequence and the horizontal line increases in length, pointing to the right and left alternately.
6 **a** The shape increases with the alternate addition of a black spot and a white circle.
7 **d** The first letter represents the position of the small circle within the larger circle (A at the top, B on the right, C at the bottom). The second letter represents the shape at the bottom of the pattern (D a triangle, E a square, F a circle).
8 **a** The first letter represents the pattern of circles around the central circle (G is no circles, H is for one circle top right, J is for one circle top left). The second letter represents the shading style of the central circle (X is white, Y is diagonal lines, Z is black).
9 **c** The first letter represents the shading style of the rectangle (N is horizontal lines, P is black, M is diagonal lines, L is white). The second letter represents the pattern of the circles at the bottom of the shape (W is a large circle on small, Y is two small circles, V is two medium sized circles, X is a small circle on top of large).
10 **b** The first letter represents the number of plus signs in the shape (A is 1, B is 2, C is 3, D is 4). The second letter represents the outer shape (X is a circle, Y is a triangle, Z is a square).
11 **e** The first letter represents the angle of the line across the hexagon (A is diagonal bottom left to top right, B is diagonal top left to bottom right, C is horizontal). The second letter represents the shading pattern (S is half black half white, T is all shaded with cross-lines, U is half shaded with cross-lines).
12 **c** The first letter represents the shape at the top of the curve line (A is a black circle, B is a white circle, C is a 'sun', D is a white 'sun'). The second letter represents the pattern of lines at the base (X is 2 lines, Y is 3 lines, Z is a zigzag).

Test 2 (pages 4–5)

1 **b** The first letter represents the direction of the arrow in the shape (A is up, B is to the right, C is down, D is to the left). The second letter represents the number of black spots (X is 4, Y is 3, Z is 1).
2 **c** The first letter represents the location of the triangle in relation to the circle (E across the circumference, D outside the circle, F inside the circle). The second letter represents the shading of the small circle (R is black, S is hatched lines, T is white).
3 **c** The first letter represents the number of lines in the zigzag excluding the edges of the square (A is 6, B is 7, C is 8). The second letter represents the shading and shape inside each square (H black square, G white square, J white circle, K black circle).
4 **c** The first letter represents the orientation of the L-shaped outline (L with right angle at top right, M with right angle at top left, N with right angle at bottom left). The second letter represents the white shape (X larger circle, Y triangle, Z smaller circle).
5 **a** The first letter represents the pattern within the small circles at each end of the triplet (A cross, B white circle, C black circle, D vertical line). The second letter represents the shape within the central circle of the triplet (X a small square, Y a small circle, Z a small triangle).
6 **d** The first letter represents the direction the arrow points (A up, B right, C down, D left). The second letter represents the shading of the circle (X white, Y half black and half white, Z black).
7 **e** The background black and white shape stays the same, the inner black and white shapes move to the outside of the larger shape.
8 **b** The arrows rotate 90° clockwise, and the arrowheads become inverted Vs and vice versa.
9 **d** The shape is divided into six parts 'cut' down the middle and twice across the shape, with the sections separated out.
10 **b** The shape is the same but smaller, with the top left white quarter shaded black, and the ×s become horizontal lines.
11 **e** The black shape becomes the shape for the main outline, and the outer dotted shape is reduced in size and goes inside the new main shape.
12 **e** The shape is rotated 180°, the white horizontal rectangle becomes black, and the black one becomes white.

Test 3 (pages 6–7)

1 **c** All the shapes in the set have a solid outside line, with a dotted inner line and a central curved shape.
2 **d** All the shapes in the set have four sides with the line style the same for all four sides.
3 **a** All of the shapes in the set have two identical small circles in the top two triangles and two ovals on the kite tail; each oval is either black or white.
4 **d** All of the shapes in the set have a thick black V-shape line, with a small black spot with four short lines.
5 **e** All of the shapes in the set have either a double plain line with a central dotted line and a black circle, or a double dotted line with a central plain line and a white circle.
6 **c** All of the curved line patterns in the set enclose four distinct spaces.
7 **e** The missing square is a reflection of the top left square in a diagonal mirror line from the bottom left of the grid to the top right.

8 **b** All the arrows point from the corner of each small square into the centre, rotating around the four corners in each row of the grid.

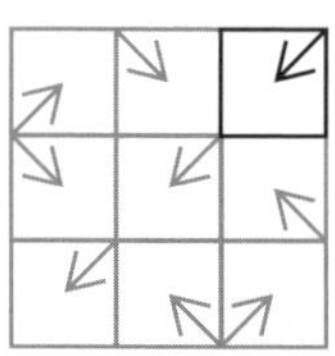

9 **a** The bottom row of the grid is the same as the top row, so the missing square will be the same as the top middle square.

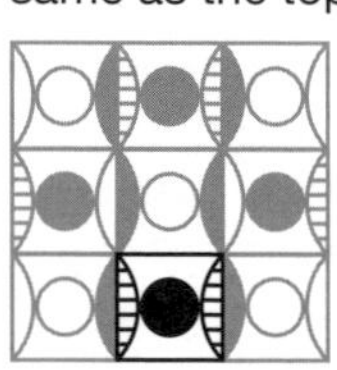

10 **c** The outer triangles of the star have an alternating pattern.

11 **e** Diagonally opposite triangles within the central hexagon of the shape are reflections of the opposite triangle.

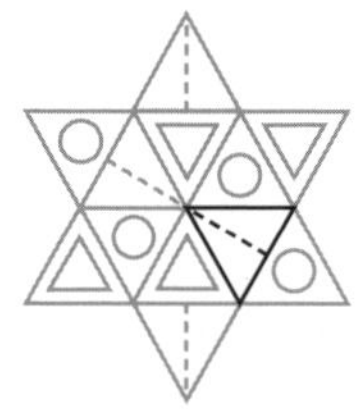

12 **d** The patterns in the triangles within the central hexagon each reflect the pattern diagonally opposite.

Test 4 (pages 8–9)

1 **a** The white oval goes up two then down one space along the sequence; the arrow alternates left then right, moving up one position in each pair.
2 **e** The C-shape of circles rotates 90° clockwise each time; there is always one large black circle in the top-right position. The colour of the three small circles alternates W–B–W and B–W–B each time.
3 **c** There are four columns in a repeating sequence so the next pattern will be the same as the third shape given in the sequence.
4 **b** The number of black circles follows the pattern 3–2–1–0–1– so the next pattern has two; the style of arrowheads at the ends of the vertical and horizontal lines alternate.
5 **c** All of the shapes have a linked triangle–square–triangle and the number of small white circles on the outside of these shapes increases by one along the sequence.
6 **d** The circle on top of the rectangle progresses along the top from left to right, the number of lines at the left end of the rectangle decreases by one as the number on the right increases by one.
7 **d** The first letter represents the shading style of the central circle (X is black, Y is striped, Z is white). The second letter represents the number of 'petals' and their shading (P is 5 white, R is 6 white, Q is 5 grey and S is 6 grey).
8 **a** The first letter represents the shading of the two small oval shapes (A both white,

B one black and one white, C both black). The second letter represents the numbers of lines (L is 2, M is 3, N is 4, O is 5).

9 **c** The first letter represents the shading style of the rectangle (A is white, B is diagonal lines, C is cross-hatched, D is grey). The second letter represents the number of shaded sections within the circle (X is 2, Y is 1).

10 **b** The first letter represents the style of the outer 'band' (E is narrow, F is wide, G is patterned). The second letter represents the position of the band around the cylinder (L at the bottom, M in the middle, N at the top).

11 **e** The first letter represents the pattern at the top of the shape (A is a single point, B is a wide shape, C is a double point). The second letter represents the style of the bottom lines (X is black pinheads, Y is white pinheads, Z is crosses).

12 **a** The first letter represents the number of white circles (C is 3, D is 4, E is 5). The second letter represents the number of black circles (W is 1, X is 2, Y is 3, Z is 4).

Test 5 (pages 10–11)

1 **c** The two ×-faces are opposite in the net so must be on opposite sides of the cube, they cannot be adjacent.

2 **e** One black face can be adjacent to the face with the black circle, but the second black face will be opposite the black circle so cannot be adjacent.

3 **b** The two faces with the double headed arrows are not adjacent in the net so cannot be adjacent in the cube.

4 **e** The face adjacent to the top of the T-face has a black circle, not the white circle.

5 **a** The face with the X is not adjacent to the white circle in the net so will be on opposite faces in the cube.

6 **d** The face with the cross and the face with the white square are not adjacent in the net so cannot be adjacent in the cube.

7 **d** All of the shapes in the set are composed of three elements.

8 **a** All of the shapes in the set have five sides.

9 **d** All of the shapes in the set have two loops with different shading styles in each loop.

10 **a** All of the shapes in the set have one straight line crossed by two straight lines.

11 **c** All of the rectangles in the set have a white border round an internal patterned smaller rectangle and they have an even fringe on one or both ends.

12 **c** All of the shapes in the set are symmetrical with a dotted line along the line of symmetry.

Test 6 (pages 12–13)

1 **c** The first letter represents the shading and relative position of the inner two circles (A is black inside white, B is black overlapping with white, C is white overlapping with white, D is white inside white). The second letter represents the outer shape of the pattern (X is a circle, Y is a triangle, Z is a square).

2 **b** The first letter represents the number of short lines (A is 2, B is 4, C is 6). The second letter represents the number of points on the stars (X is 4, Y is 5, Z is 6).

3 **b** The first letter represents the colour and shape at the top of the 'flagpole' (D a black oval, E a white oval, F a white diamond). The second letter represents the number of sections in the 'flag' (L is 2, M is 3, N is 4).

4 **a** The first letter represents the number of sections in the rectangles (S is 4, T is 3). The second letter represents the shading style of the circle (E is black, F is +, G is cross-hatched, H is ≡).

5 **d** The first letter represents the shapes (P for triangles, Q for quadrilaterals). The second letter represents the position of the dotted line shape in relation to the plain line shape (N is above, S is below, E to the right, W to the left).

6 **c** The first letter represents the pattern in the corner squares (A is white circle, B is black circle, C is black square, D is an ×). The second letter represents the pattern of the central square (E is white circle, F is black circle, G is black square, H is an ×).

7 **d** The inner white shapes become smaller and black, the number remains the same.

8 **d** The number of loops in the coil gives the number of zigzag elements along the line.

9 **e** Working from the bottom of the pattern the lowest shape goes inside the shape above, which is inside the one above it, etc.

10 **a** The pattern is rotated 180°, the white circles become black on long lines and the arrowheads are inverted on shortened lines.

11 **b** The elongated outer shape is 'squashed' so the oval becomes a circle; the inner shapes are also squashed to becomes squares and their shading changes to black).

12 **e** The shape is reflected with the shading styles changing from lines to black and vice versa.

Test 7 (pages 14–15)

1 **c** The corners of the shape become rounded, the white sections become black and vice versa.
2 **e** The arrow is rotated through 180°, the white outlines become a black dotted line with a black arrowhead.
3 **b** The top shape moves inside the middle shape, which moves inside the bottom shape.
4 **d** The individual cubes are placed together to form a regular cuboid on a horizontal plane.
5 **a** The line of shapes rotates 45° clockwise to a vertical position and becomes two lines. The black shapes become white with small white circles inside in the first column; the black shapes become white and vice versa in the second column.
6 **d** The shape stays the same but is reduced in size; the number of sections in the large shape gives the number of the smaller shapes; the shading style of each section of the large shape is replicated in one of the smaller shapes.
7 **d** The two faces with white circles are not adjacent and must be on opposite sides of the cube.
8 **e** The face with the grey lined square and the face with black square must be on opposite sides of the cube.
9 **c** The faces with the white circles are in a line with the face with the black circle so the black circle cannot be adjacent to both white circles when in a cube.
10 **b** The two black faces are on faces that will be on opposite sides of the cube so they cannot be adjacent.
11 **c** One of the faces with an × is opposite the face with the white circle so there cannot be two faces with × adjacent to the face with the white circle.
12 **a** One of the faces with a black spot will be adjacent to the bottom edge of the face with the black arrow, that is below the arrow not next to it; the other face with a black spot will be opposite the face with the arrow.

Test 8 (pages 16–17)

1 **a** Curved lines with black circles and an open arrowhead alternate with curved lines with white circles and closed white arrowheads and the number of circles increases every second shape.
2 **c** The number of small squares cut out of the sides of the rectangle increases by one each time and the shading of the strip on the left of the rectangle follows the sequence: diagonal lines–black–horizontal lines–.
3 **a** The number of black spots in the upper oval decreases by one each time, the number of black spots in the lower oval increases by one each time and the three crosses alternate between the lower and upper oval.
4 **a** The shaded segment of the circle moves clockwise one place round the circle each time, the black spots increase by one each time, occupying the segments ahead of the progressing shaded segment.
5 **b** The number of small squares decreases by one each time, starting from the bottom side, then from the right side and then from the top.
6 **d** The black line across the rectangular bar moves progressively from left to right, the number of beads on the curved line increases by one each time, alternately adding a black or white bead to the bottom of the 'thread'.
7 **e** All of the shapes in the set are circles with black arrowheads projecting from them.
8 **a** All of the shapes in the set are made up of three overlapping circles of the same size, with the three sections where two circles overlap shaded.
9 **b** All of the shapes in the set are made up of single longer line crossed by two shorter lines of equal-length.
10 **b** All of the shapes in the set are ovals or circles with an inner shaded oval or circle; they all have six short lines projecting from them.
11 **e** All of the shapes in the set have the same shape on the outer pointed tip of the 'comma' as the shape in the middle; the outer shape is black and the inner one is white.
12 **d** All of the shapes in the set are regular three-dimensional solids with no dotted lines.

Test 9 (pages 18–19)

1 **b** The shape is rotated by 180°, the white element becomes black and the black becomes white with a line and the vertical shading of the third section becomes horizontal line shading.
2 **b** The one shape becomes a set of four identical shapes with the white shape at the right end becoming black at the end of each of the four, and there is no white shape at the left end of the four small shapes.
3 **b** The vertical arrows become vertical black bars and the vertical black bars become vertical arrows with black arrowheads.

4 **d** The first shape is reduced in size and placed in a circle, the cross hatch shading becomes diagonal top left to bottom right shading in the inner shape with shading from bottom left to top right in the surrounding circle.
5 **e** The number of circles with a cross gives the number of circles in the second part and alternate circles have diagonal line shading in opposite directions.
6 **a** The shape of the two faces shown of the 3D solid become two 2D shapes linked by a curved line.
7 **a** All of the shapes in the set are either squares with a triangle inside, or triangles with squares inside and the inner shape is always black.
8 **e** All of the shapes in the set are comprised of three elements.
9 **c** All of the shapes in the set are made up of an overlapping square and circle.
10 **b** All of the shapes in the set are arrows pointing to the top right (NE) and they all have just one arrowhead.
11 **d** All of the shapes in the set are made up of rectangles containing two smaller, equal rectangles.
12 **c** All of the shapes in the set are made up of ovals, within each oval and touching its inner edge, is a small white circle with a central black spot.

Test 10 (pages 20–21)

1 **a** The first letter represents the number of sections within the rectangle (X is 4, Y is 3, Z is 2). The second letter represents the pattern along the short sides of the rectangle (L is triangles, M is short lines, N is semi-circles).
2 **c** The first letter represents the style of the double lines (L is outer line plain with inner line dotted, M is outer dotted and inner plain, N is both plain, O is both dotted). The second letter represents the arrow style and orientation (D is white arrow pointing out, E is white arrow pointing in, F is black arrow pointing out, G is black arrow pointing in).
3 **e** The first letter represents the colour combination of the circles in the pattern (A is all black, B is all white, C is black and white). The second letter represents the total number of circles (T is 2, U is 3, V is 4).
4 **b** The first letter represents the number and position of the short lines (D is three vertical lines, E is two vertical and one horizontal, F is four vertical, G is four vertical and one horizontal). The second letter represents the style of the circle (A is white with thin line, B is white with thick black line, C is black).
5 **e** The first letter represents the shading pattern of the first rectangle in each pattern (L is line shaded at the ends and black in the middle, M is white at the ends with line shaded in the middle, N is black at the ends with line shaded in the middle). The second letter represents the relative position of the second rectangle to the first one (X is level, Y is mid-way down, Z is the below).
6 **d** The first letter represents the shape surrounding the black spots and the number of spots in the shape (A is large circle with two spots, B is small circle with two spots, C is rectangle with two spots, D is a large circle with four spots). The second letter represents the outer shape (F is a circle, G is a square, H is an octagon).
7 **d** The two faces with arrows are projecting out on opposite sides of the net so they must be opposite in the cube.
8 **e** One of the faces with a cross will be adjacent to the face with a white circle, but the second face with a cross will be opposite the white circle face, so they cannot both be adjacent to the white circle face in the cube.
9 **c** The face with cross hatched shading and the white face are not adjacent in the net so cannot be adjacent in the cube.
10 **c** When one of the faces with diagonal lines is at the front of the cube with the black square at the top, the face to the right must either be the cross or the other face with diagonal lines, the white circle cannot be adjacent on the right.
11 **e** The face with the cross is opposite the face with the black circle, so they cannot be adjacent in the cube.
12 **b** The face with the equilateral triangle has the base of the triangle parallel to the edge shared with the face with the white circle.

Test 11 (pages 22–23)

1 **d** All of the shapes in the set have two crossed lines, with both lines the same style and with a black spot at one end of one line.
2 **d** All of the shapes in the set are solid drawn with no dotted lines and with one flat plain face shaded grey.
3 **e** All of the shapes in the set are made up of two different shapes linked by a curvy line that has one loop in it.
4 **b** The overlapping squares at the bottom right of the shape reduce in number by one each time and the white circles on the curved lines from the top left corner increase by one each time.

5 **d** The black spot follows the pattern down two steps, up one, the white circle moves progressively up but 'underneath' the 'steps' on the inside and, after reaching the top, starts again at the bottom.

6 **b** The pattern of shapes is repeated in alternate squares, the shapes are white in the first two squares, then black in the next two, then white, etc.

7 **a** The line pattern remains the same, the white spots become black and vice versa.

8 **e** The outer elongated shape is made 'regular' so the oval becomes a circle and the rectangle becomes a square; the converse happens to the three inner shapes, which retain their original shading.

9 **b** The white circles and crosses in the inner shape move to the outer part of the square and the black circles in the outer part move into the inner shape, the numbers of each do not change.

10 **a** The first letter represents the number and colour of the large circles (A is none, B is one black, C is two white, D is two black). The second letter represents the total number of small circles (X is 5, Y is 6, Z is 7).

11 **a** The first letter represents the style and number of the longer arrows (A is 4 long lines with arrowheads, B is 4 long lines with Vs, C is 6 long lines with arrowheads, D is 6 long lines with Vs at the end of each); the second letter represents the style of the short lines (X is with Vs at the end, Y has plain lines, Z has arrowheads).

12 **d** The first letter represents the size and colour of the square (L is large black, M is large white, N is small black, O is small white). The second letter represents the number of circles in the shape (X is 3, Y is 4, Z is 5).

Test 12 (pages 24–25)

1 **c** The grid increases to the right by adding horizontal and vertical lines alternately, with a decreasing number of squares in each column.

2 **a** The number of cubes in the shape increases by one each time, with the colours of the circles and side faces changing in alternate patterns.

3 **d** The shape rotates 90° clockwise each time and the two triangles alternate from black to white.

4 **d** The face with the double ended arrow points to the face with the cross and at the other end points to the black face, it does not point to the face with the black circle.

5 **e** Two of the faces with the white circles are opposite each other so cannot be adjacent in the cube.

6 **d** The face with the black circle is opposite the face with the white circle so cannot be adjacent in the cube.

7 **c**

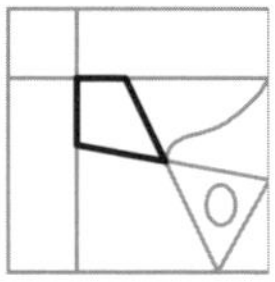

8 **d**

9 **e**

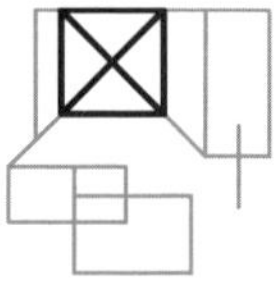

10 **a** The first letter represents the shape at the top of the pattern (L is circle with cross, K is square with single vertical line, M is circle with single vertical line, N is square with cross). The second letter represents the pattern of the base lines (A is three separate short lines, B is three lines joined at the left, C is three lines joined at the right).

11 **c** The first letter represents the direction of the arrow projecting from the circle (E is up, F is right, G is down, H is left). The second letter represents the style of the circle (X has a double line, Y has a single line).

12 **a** The first letter represents the number of triangles in the pattern (A is 3, B is 2 and C is 1). The second letter relates to the shading (P has black shading, Q has diagonal lines, R has no shading, S has grey shading).

Test 13 (pages 26–27)

1 **a** The line shape at the bottom of the pattern changes into a 3D container shape, the 'flower' pattern loses the line and is added to the side to the 'container'.

2 **c** The pattern in the bottom right square is repeated in all of the sections of the grid.

3 **d** The lines given form the sides of a regular 2D shape, retaining the lines or arrowheads at their ends, which project beyond the vertices of the shape.

4 **d** All of the shapes in the set have four 'loops' that project outwards.

5 **d** All of the shapes in the set have one

triangular tip projecting from the circle, and one band of pattern around the circle.

6 **e** All of the patterns in the set only have right-angled turns and only enclose one area.

7 **c**

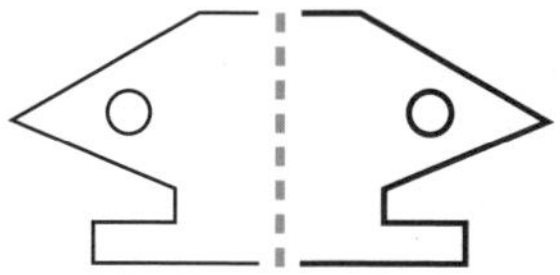

8 **a**

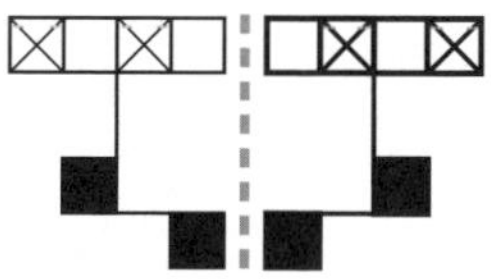

9 **b**

10 **d** The number of loops at the top of the curved line increases by one along the sequence and the number of small white circles decreases by one.

11 **e** The small black line at the right hand end of the top line moves to the left along the sequence, the black shaded rectangle in the bar moves one place to the right and the zigzag line at the bottom has an additional line added.

12 **a** The squares and circles alternate; in the squares, the small black circles in the lower left decrease by one and the number of L-shape lines in the top left increase by one along the sequence.

Test 14 (pages 28–29)

1 **e** The number of sides gives the number of horizontal lines and the white small shapes become black at the end of each line.

2 **c** The outer plain-lined shape only is reflected in a vertical line of reflection, the original plain outer line becomes dotted and the inner shape remains unchanged.

3 **a** The whole pattern is rotated 180° and the black shaded shape becomes white.

4 **d** All of the shapes in the set have two rounded projections and two rounded indentations.

5 **e** All of the shapes in the set are made up of five black dots with short lines between them.

6 **d** All of the patterns in the set comprise three elements.

7 **c** The first letter represents the number of small circles (A is 1, B is 2, C is none). The second letter represents the position of the black circle in the column of circles (X is at the top, Y is in the middle, Z is at the bottom).

8 **b** The first letter represents the style of the rectangle (A tall and narrow, B square, C short and narrow, D short and wide). The second letter represents the shading of the circle (X is white, Y is diagonal lines, Z is black).

9 **a** The first letter represents the number of the arrow/pin shapes crossing the outline (E is 3, F is 4, G is 5). The second letter represents the shape and shading at the end of the short lines (U is white circle, V is black triangle, S is simple arrow, T is black circle).

10 **b** The face with the cross is opposite one of the faces with a white circle, and adjacent to the other, so it cannot be adjacent to both when in a cube.

11 **c** The half black/half white face is not adjacent to the face with the back circle in the net and must be on opposite faces in the cube, not adjacent.

12 **e** The two faces with the white circles are not adjacent in the net and so will be on opposite faces in the cube.

Test 15 (pages 30–31)

1 **d** The number of white circles decreases by one, the number of short vertical lines along the bottom increase by one and the position of the arrowhead and tail alternate.

2 **c** There is one less L-shape line in successive patterns along the sequence.

3 **e** The white circle moves along the pattern, alternating between being on top or below the rectangle, the black bar moves to the left two places, then back one to the right, then two to the left, etc.

4 **b** The first letter represents the orientation of the T element of the pattern (A has the 'junction' of the T at the top, B has it on the right, C has it on the bottom, D has it on the left). The second letter represents the style of the diagonal lines/arrows (X the arrows point inwards, Y the arrows point outwards, Z plain lines with no arrowhead).

5 **b** The first letter represents the style and number of the patterns on the corners of the squares (L two black spots with lines, M four black spots with lines, N two corners each with three lines, P four corners each with three lines). The second letter represents the central shape (S is a white circle, T is a cross-hatched circle, U is a black circle, V is a square).

6 **a** The first letter represents the small shapes around the large circle (X is white circles, Y is black circles, Z is black triangles). The second

letter represents the direction of the arrow (A is to the left, B is to the top, C is to the right, D is to the bottom).

7 **e**

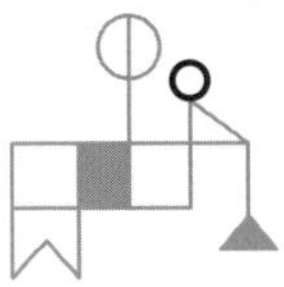

8 **c**

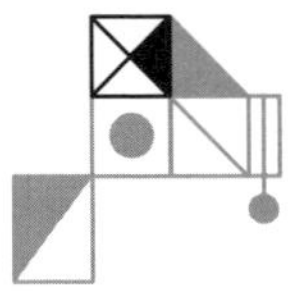

9 **c**

10 **e** All of the shapes in the set have five sides, with one black and one white circle inside them.

11 **d** All of the shapes in the set have a small white circle inside them and a small black circle on the outside, touching one of the corners

12 **d** All of the shapes in the set have a zigzag comprising five lines and one end has a black dot and the other end has a T-end.

Test 16 (pages 32–33)

1 **c** The face with the large X is opposite the white face in the net so cannot be adjacent in the cube.

2 **e** The face with the circle containing the cross is not adjacent to the face with the white circle in the net so they cannot be adjacent in the cube.

3 **b** When the face with the black square is at the top and the face with the candle is at the front, with the candle the right way up, then the face to the right must be the circle with a black spot.

4 **e** The shape at the top is repeated to make a column of three, with inverse shading in the top and bottom shape.

5 **b** The shape is rotated 90° clockwise and the white circle becomes black.

6 **a** The missing shape is made up of the top left quarter containing the pattern of shapes from the original bottom right quarter.

7 **e** All of the shapes in the set have two triangles joined by a short line, one triangle is all black and the other triangle is black with a white band along two of the three sides.

8 **d** All of the shapes in the set have one circle and two crosses all linked on a straight line.

9 **b** All of the shapes in the set are divided into quarters, with one quarter black, one lined and two white.

10 **c**

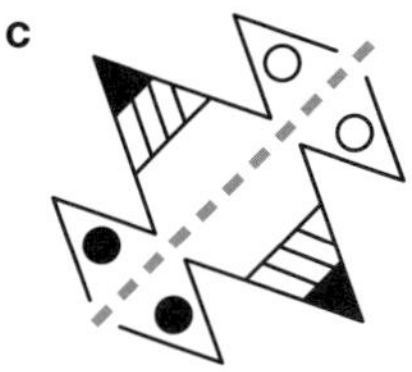

11 **b**

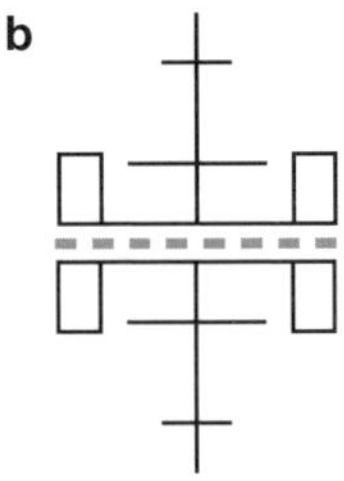

12 **e**

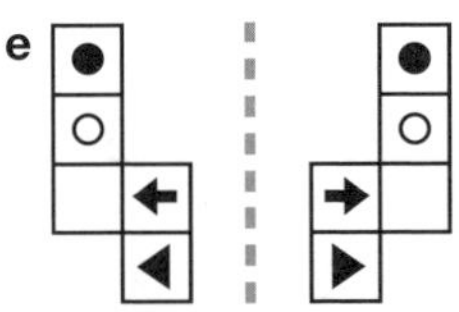

Test 17 (pages 34–35)

1 **c** The first letter represents the number of sections shaded black (A is 1, B is 2, C is 3, D is 6). The second letter represents the outer shapes (X is a circle/6-pointed star, Y is a hexagon/circle).

2 **d** The first letter represents where the horizontal line crosses the vertical line (A near the bottom, B near the top, C in the middle). The second letter represents the end shapes on the horizontal lines (S is black circle and black triangle, T is two black triangles, U is two white triangles, V is two black circles).

3 **b** The first letter represents the number of sides of the shape (L is 4, M is 5, N is 6). The second letter represents the number of black spots inside the shape (A is 3, B is 4, C is 5, D is 6).

4 **a** Each square is changed into three small circles with the middle circle projecting slightly to the right; each of the three groups of three circles replicates the shading patterns of the three squares.

5 **e** The straight lines change to a curved line in the same direction; the triangle at one end becomes a short line; the simple arrowhead becomes a solid black triangle.

6 **b** The outline shape becomes regular and the total number of circles gives the number of crosses inside the new shape.

7 **e** This is a repeating sequence of four patterns. The missing seventh shape will be the same as the third.

8 **c** The circle in the upper part of the oval alternates from white to black and the shape at the bottom follows a repeating pattern: black circle–black rectangle–striped circle– etc.

9 **d** The number of lines at the base decreases by one along the sequence, the angle between the diagonal line and the vertical increases each time and the black and white circles alternate.

10 **d** All of the shapes in the set have a semi-circle with a line from the curved edge joining the mid-point of one side of a square.

11 **b** All of the shapes in the set have a curved shape with diagonal shading, touching the edge of a black 2D shape with straight sides.

12 **e** All of the kite shapes in the set have a vertical line from top to bottom and one bow/flag on the attached 'string'.

Test 18 (pages 36–37)

1 **b** The first letter represents the number of black circles (A is 3, B is 2, C is 1, D is none). The second letter represents the number of triangles (X is 3, Y is 4, Z is 5).

2 **c** The first letter represents the direction that the arrow is pointing (F is up, G is to the right, H is down). The second letter represents the colour and position of the circles in relation to the U-shape (P is white and inside, Q is white and outside, R is black and inside, S is black and outside).

3 **d** The first letter represents the number of curly lines in the shape (A is 4, B is 3, C is 2). The second letter represents the number of points in the pattern where two lines cross (J is 3, K is 4, L is 5, M is 6).

4 **e** The top and the bottom shapes within the pattern are reflected is a vertical mirror line; the middle shape has its shading pattern reversed.

5 **d** The shape is rotated 180° and all of the dotted lines become solid lines.

6 **e** The curved arrows becomes straight arrows, the black triangular ends become simple arrowheads and the vertical shading lines become horizontal.

7 **d** The number of blocks in the rectangle decreases by one; the arrow alternates between being black and on the right, with a simple arrow on the left; and the circle alternates between being black and at the bottom with being white and at the top.

8 **a** One 'bead' or 'bar' on the top line moves from the left to the right each time, the white oval at the bottom also moves along from left to right.

9 **a** The shading of the oval alternates between small black oval within a white oval and solid black; the number of crossing points along the loopy curved line decreases by one each time.

10 **d** The face joining the bottom edge of the face with the 'T' has the circle on it not a square.

11 **e** The two faces each with two dots are not adjacent in the net and will be opposite each other in the cube, not adjacent.

12 **e** The face with the large cross and the face with the 'smiley face' are not adjacent in the net so cannot be adjacent in the cube.

Test 19 (pages 38–39)

1 **c** All of the patterns in the set have an 'H' shape with the top section enclosed and shaded; the base of the 'legs' of the H shapes have two small rectangles, one each side.

2 **e** All of the patterns in the set have five small lines within each 'bristle'.

3 **a** All of the patterns in the set have four white circles and two crosses.

4 **c**

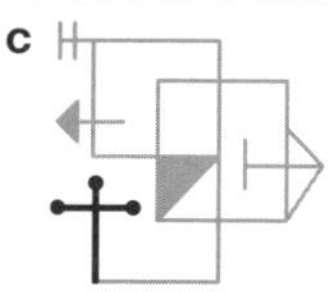

5 **e**

6 **b**

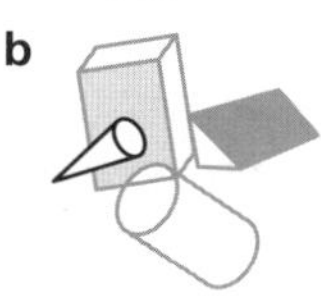

7 **b** The first letter represents the style of the white end of the shape (A is a white semi-circle with a forked line, B is a white semi-circle with an arrow, C is a white circle with an arrow, D is a white circle with a forked line). The second letter represents the style of the black end of the shape (X is a black triangle with a line, Y is a black semi-circle with two lines, Z is a black bar with two lines).

8 **a** The first letter represents the colour and size of the central square (E is large black, F is large white, G is small black, H is small white). The second letter represents the number of small squares with white circles in them (X is 1, Y is 2, Z is 3).

9 **e** The first letter represents the arrangement of the two thick black lines (A has one horizontal and one vertical, B both lines horizontal, C both lines vertical). The second letter represents the number of intersections in the pattern (X has 2, Y has 3 Z has 4).

10 **d**

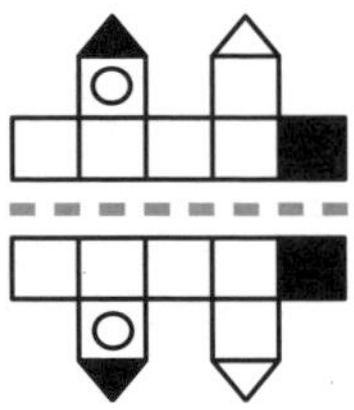

11 **a**

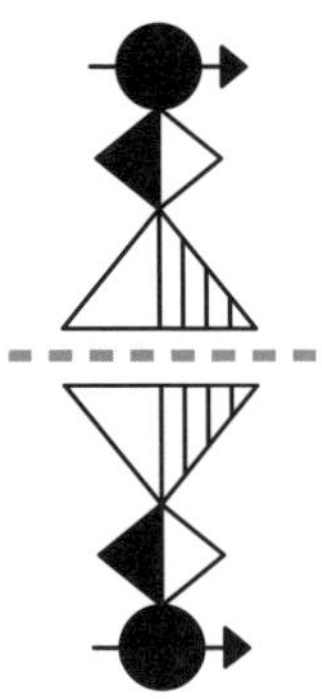

12 **c**

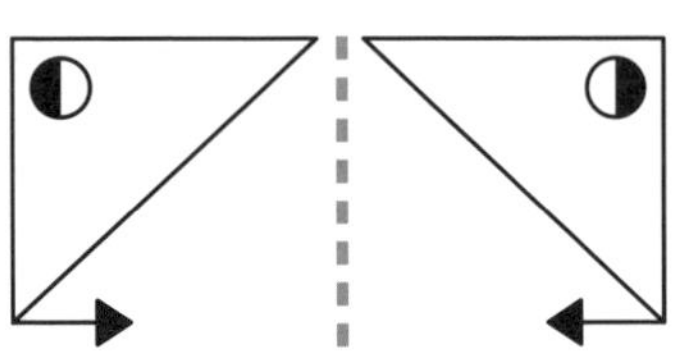

Test 20 (pages 40–41)

1 **d** The angle between the two radii in the circle increases each time and the black circle alternates between the second and fourth position.

2 **b** The sequence of shapes from left to right along each row in turn is: triangle–circle–square–rectangle–etc.; the shapes in the bottom row of the grid are each divided into four sections.

3 **a** The number of black dots at the top increases by one, the arrow alternates between pointing down and pointing up while progressing along the shape from left to right and the horizontal line alternates between solid and dotted.

4 **a** The 3D solid becomes a simple 2D face, the small shapes on the face switch from square to circle and vice versa and so does their black/white colour.

5 **b** The base of the 3D shape is drawn as a 2D shape and shaded black.

6 **c** The white squares become short black rectangles projecting on parallel lines, and the black spots that point down become white circles projecting to the right in line with the rectangles.

7 **e** The base edges of both faces with black equilateral triangles will be adjacent to the face with the cross and not the face with the white circle.

8 **c** The black face and the diagonally shaded face are not adjacent in the net, they will be opposite each other in the cube, not adjacent.

9 **a** The face with the arrow has the arrow pointing towards the face with the white circle not away from it.

10 **e** All of the shapes in the set have either three or five sides and only regular diagonal-line shading and black shading within them.

11 **c** All of the shapes in the set are cylinders, with a black circle in the middle of the circular face and a pattern of black and white bands around the cylinder.

12 **d** The patterns with the set all have a double headed straight arrow, a straight line with inverted arrowheads each end and a wavy line with a single black arrowhead.

Puzzle 1 (pages)

A

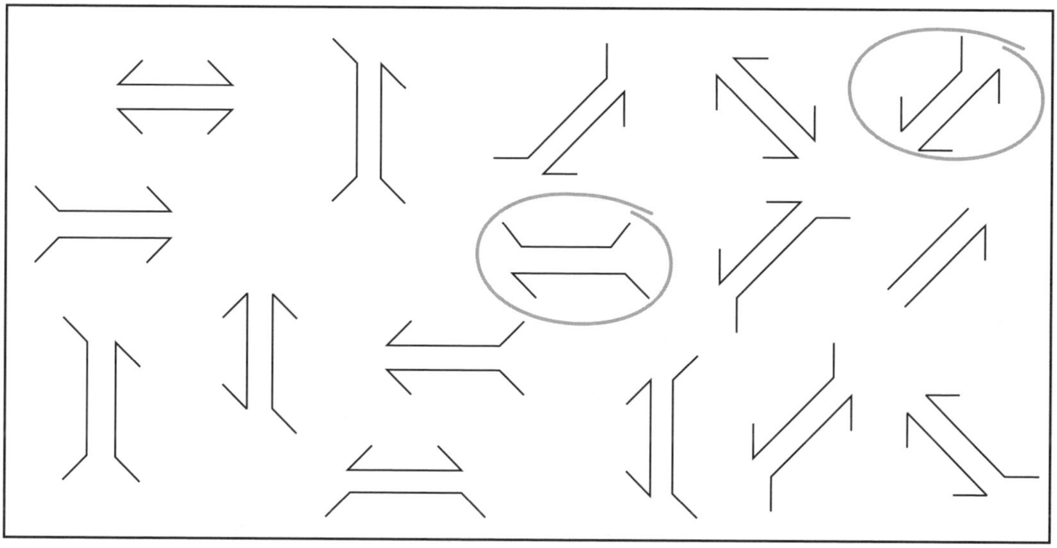

B

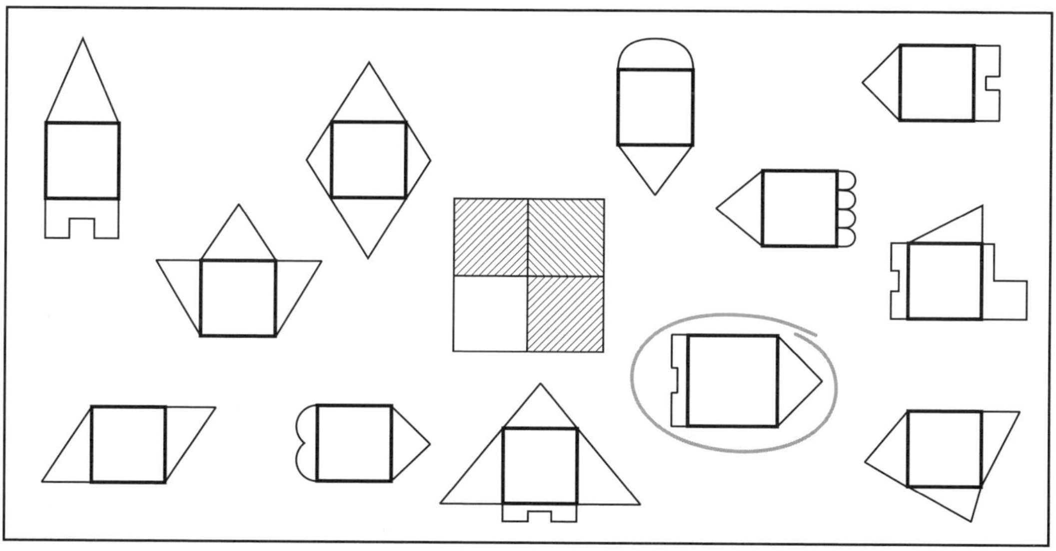

Puzzle 2 (pages)

A d
B c
C f
D g
E h
F c

Puzzle 3 (pages)

A c
B d
C b
D c
E d
F b

Puzzle 4 (pages)

A

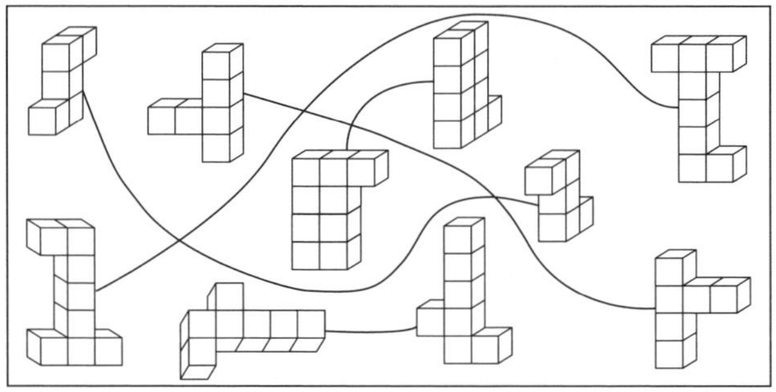

B

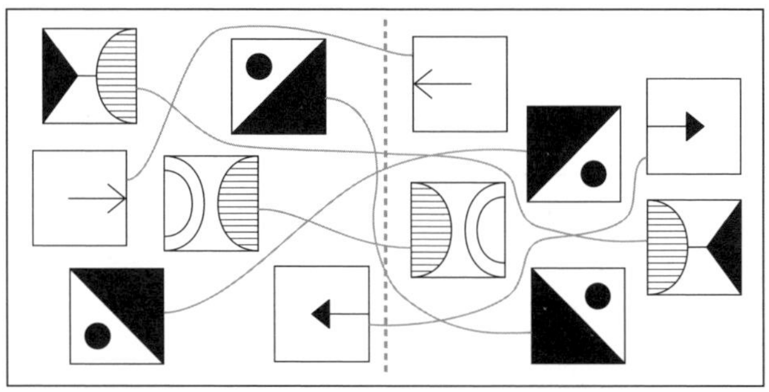

Puzzle 5 (pages)

A

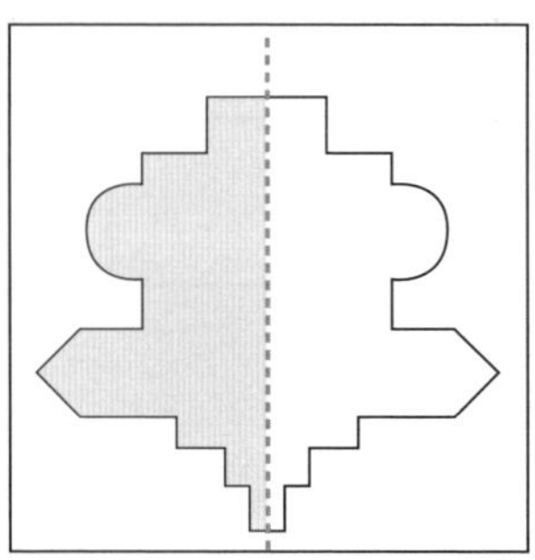

B

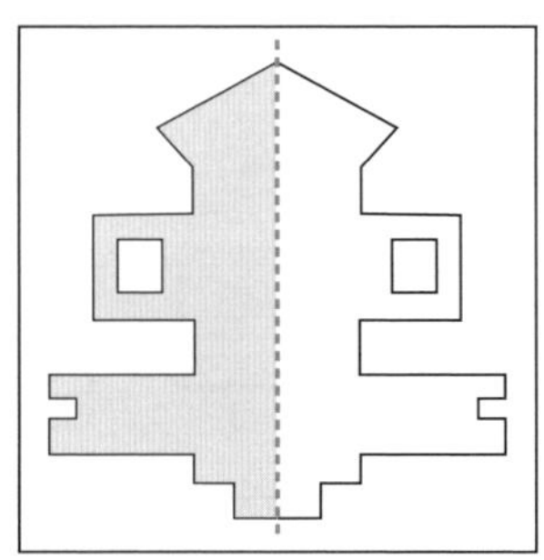

C

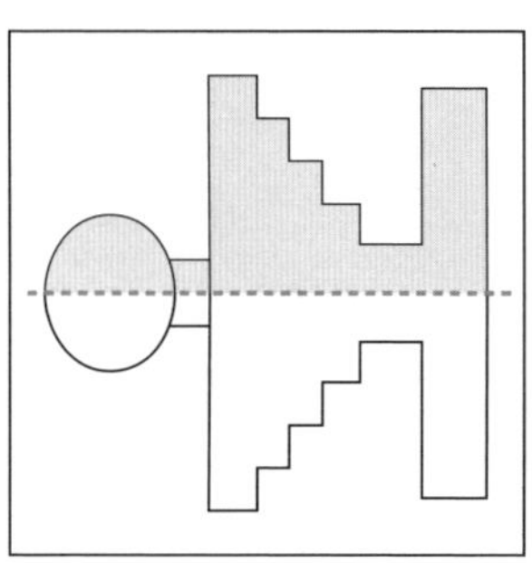

D

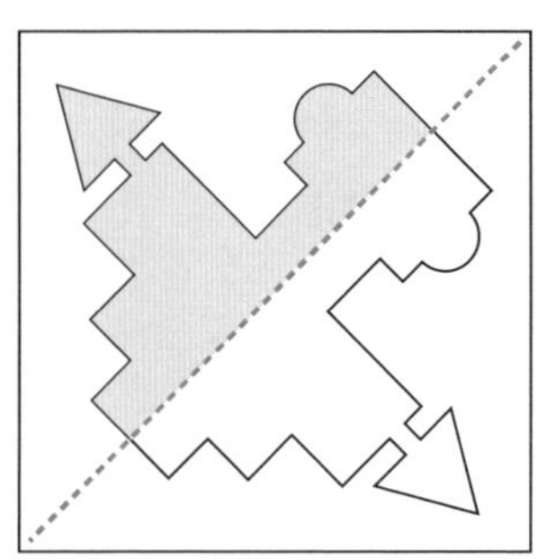

In which of the patterns is the given shape hidden?

Example

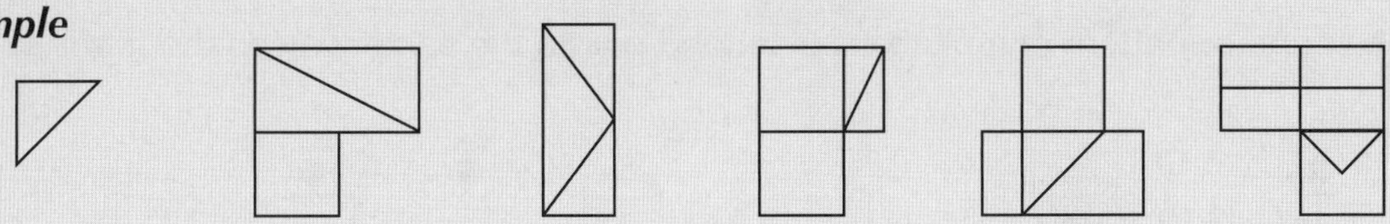

a b c (d) e

7

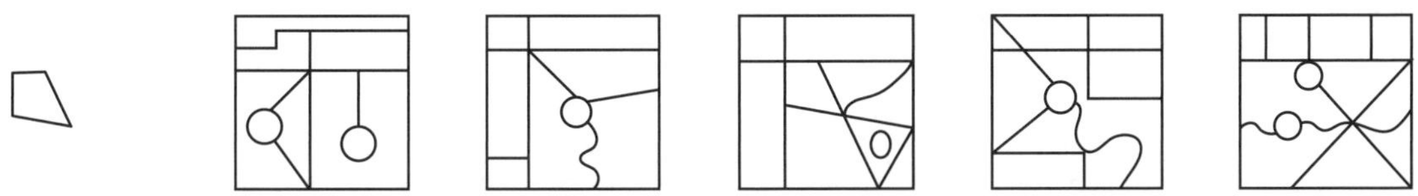

a b c d e

8

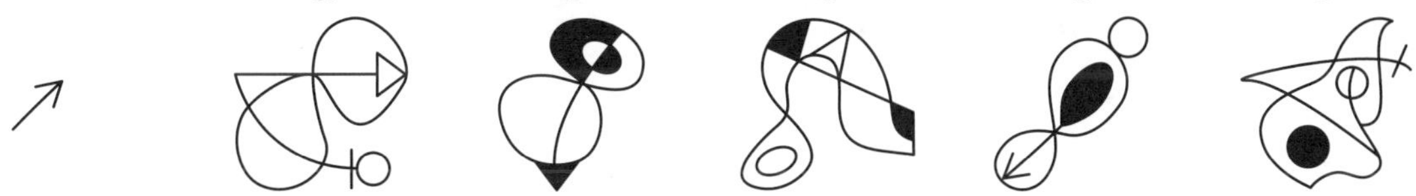

a b c d e

9

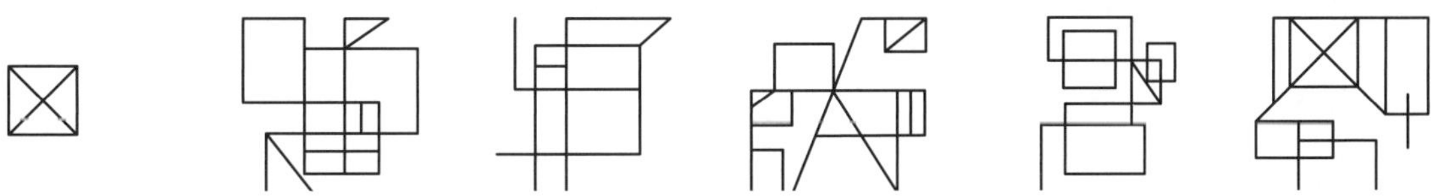

a b c d e

Using the given patterns and codes, select the code that matches the last pattern.

10

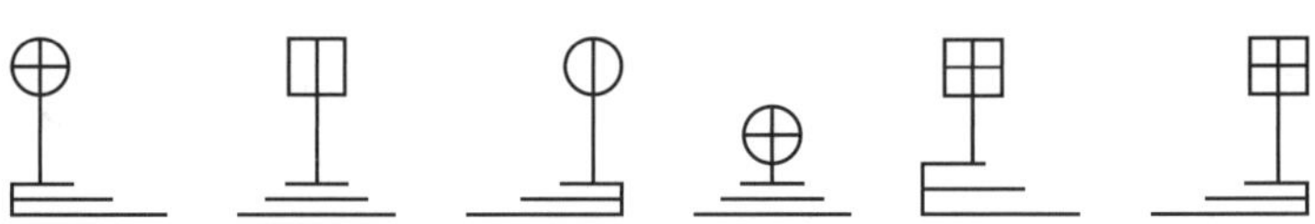

LB KA MC LA NB ?

NC	LC	NA	KC	MB
a	b	c	d	e

11

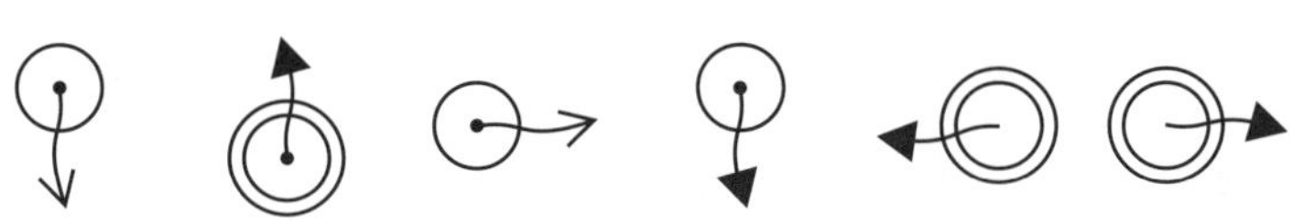

GY EX FY GX HX ?

FY	EY	FX	GX	HY
a	b	c	d	e

12

AP CP BQ BR CS ?

CQ	AQ	BP	AS	CR
a	b	c	d	e

Test 13: Mixed

Test time: 0 5 10 minutes

Which shape or pattern completes the second pair in the same way as the first pair?

1

a b c d e

2

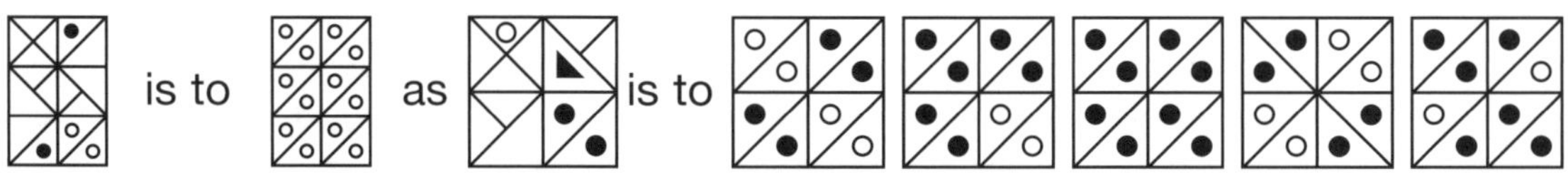

a b c d e

3

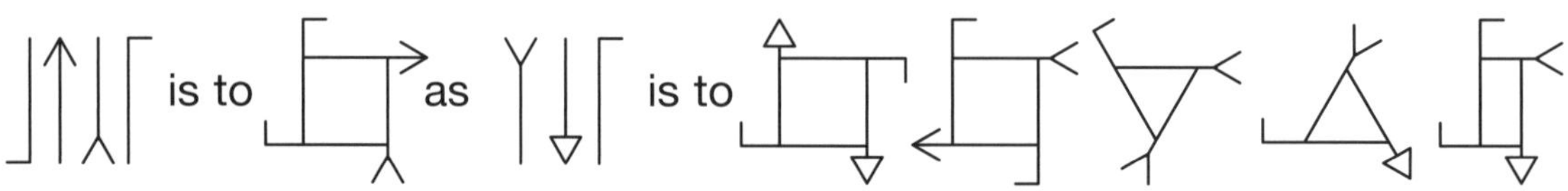

a b c d e

Which shape on the right goes best with the shapes on the left?

4

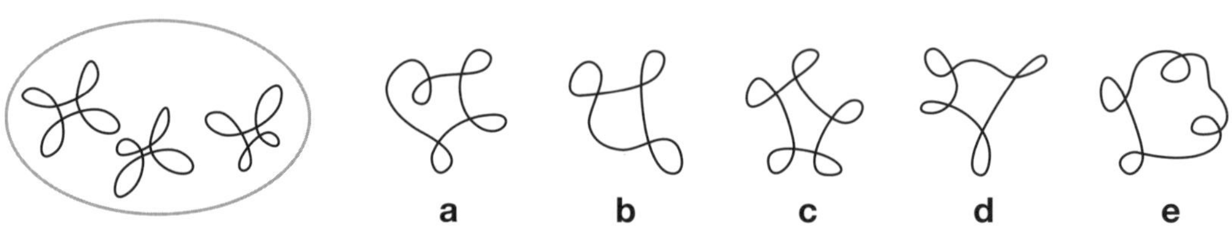

a b c d e

5

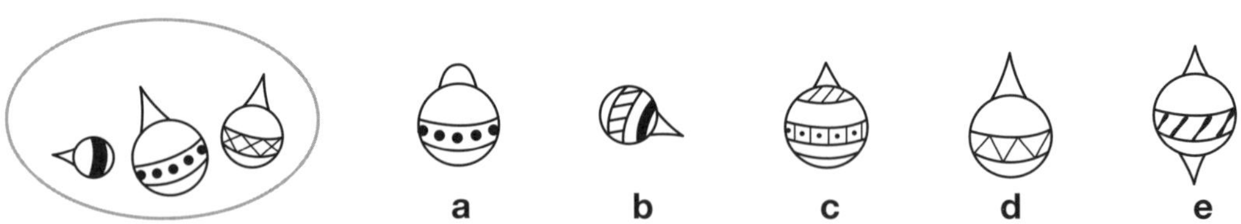

a b c d e

6

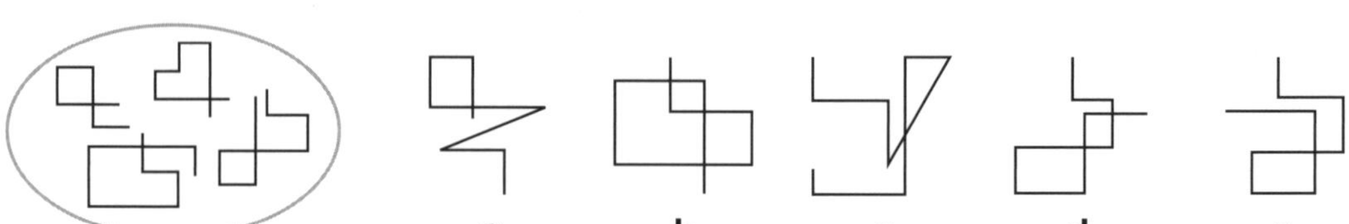

a b c d e

Which is the mirror image of the shape on the left?

Example

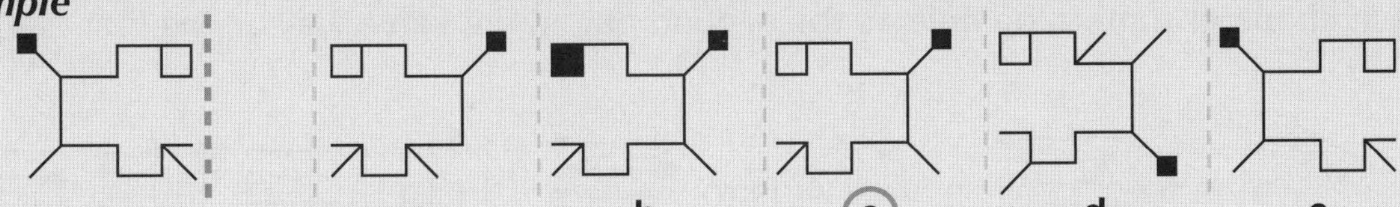

a b (c) d e

7

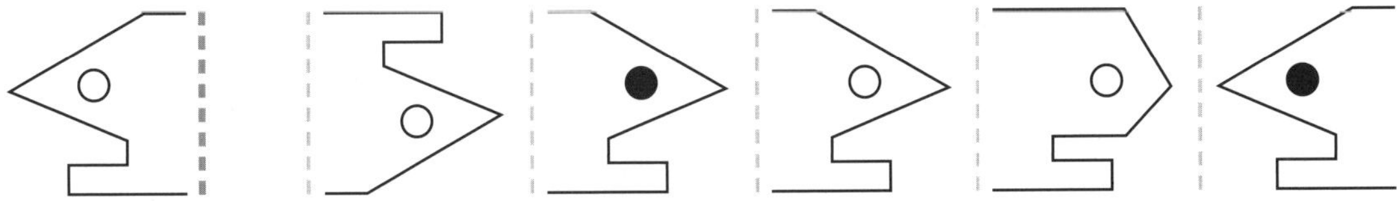

a b c d e

8

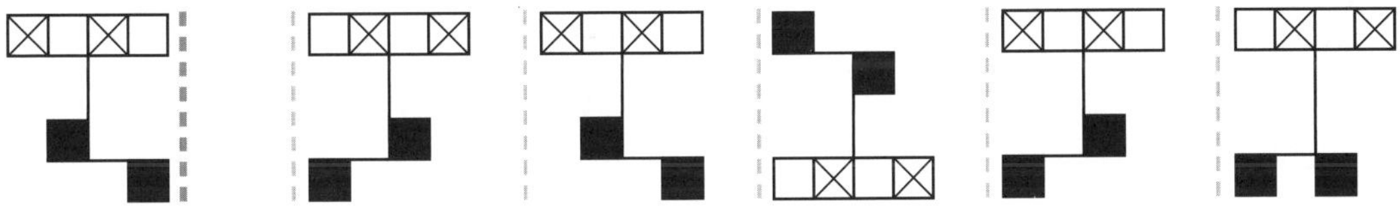

a b c d e

9

a b c d e

Which pattern continues or completes the given series?

10

a b c d e

11

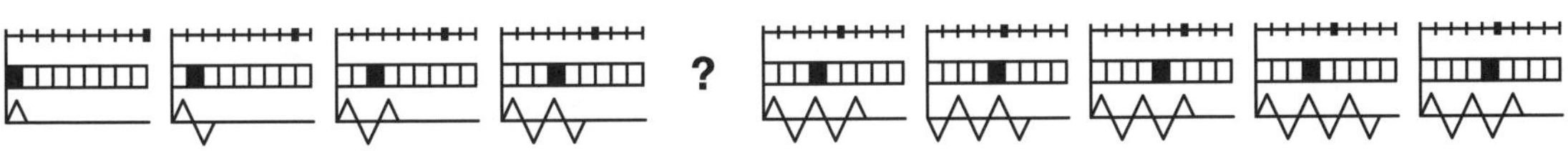

a b c d e

12

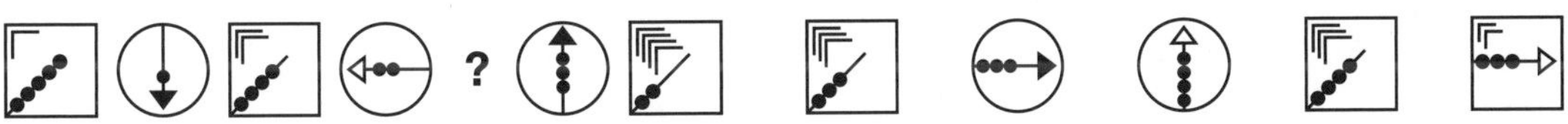

a b c d e

Total

Test 14: Mixed

Test time: 0 5 10 minutes

Which shape or pattern completes the second pair in the same way as the first pair?

1

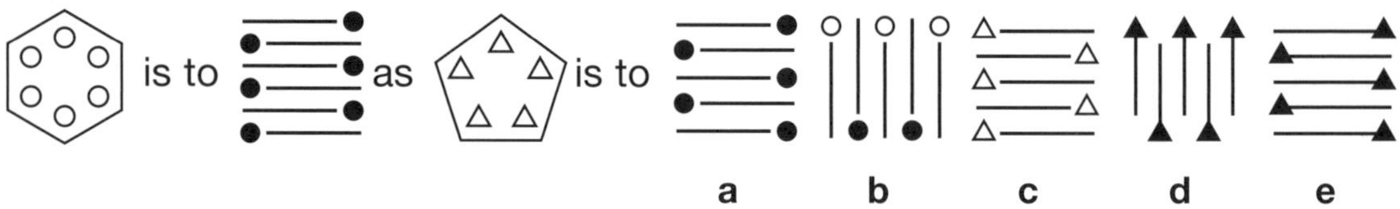

2

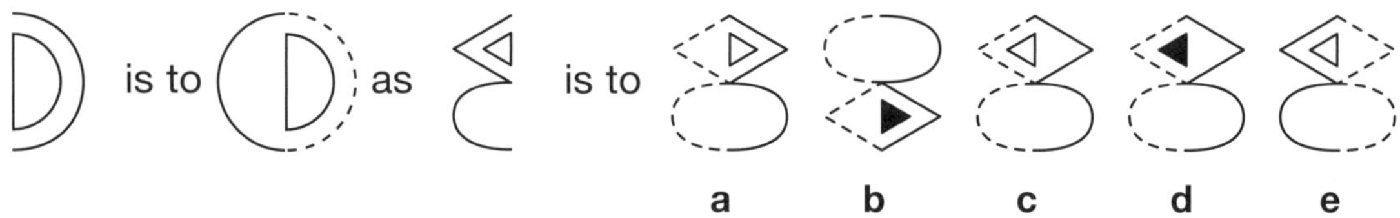

3

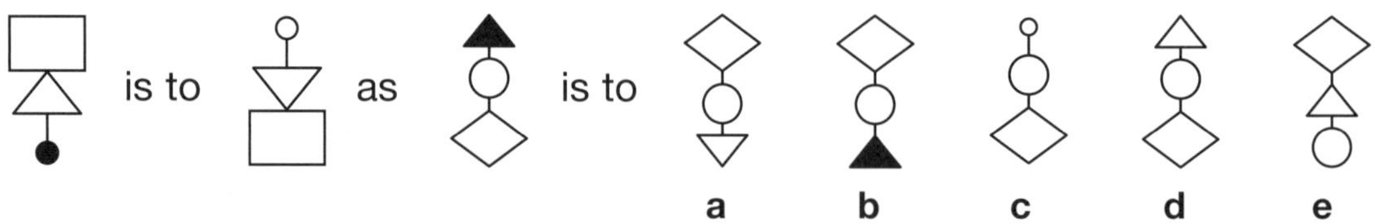

Which shape on the right goes best with the shapes on the left?

4

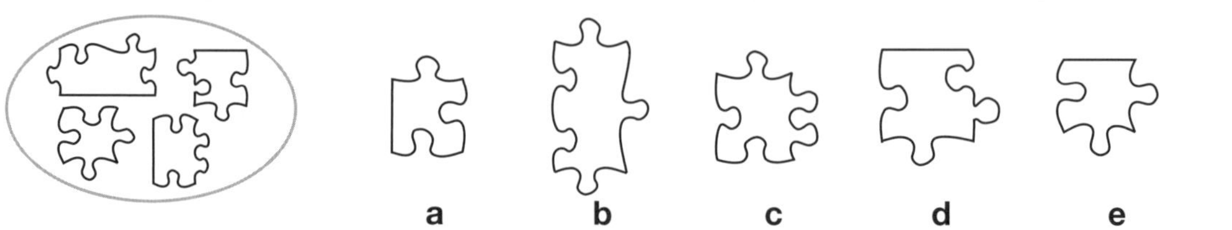

5

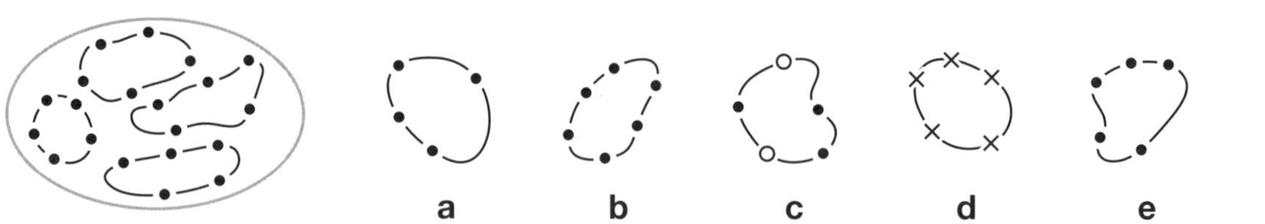

6

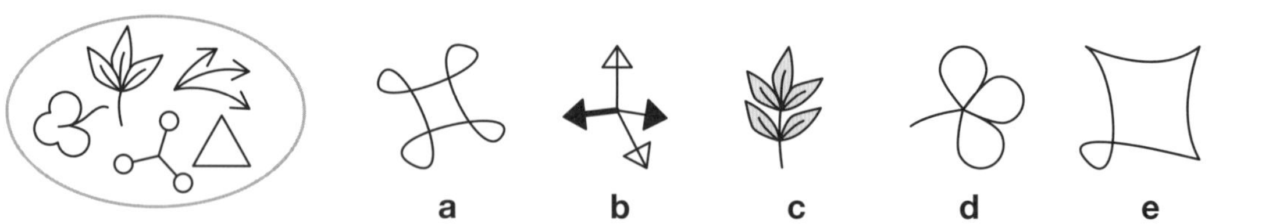

Using the given patterns and codes, select the code that matches the last pattern.

7

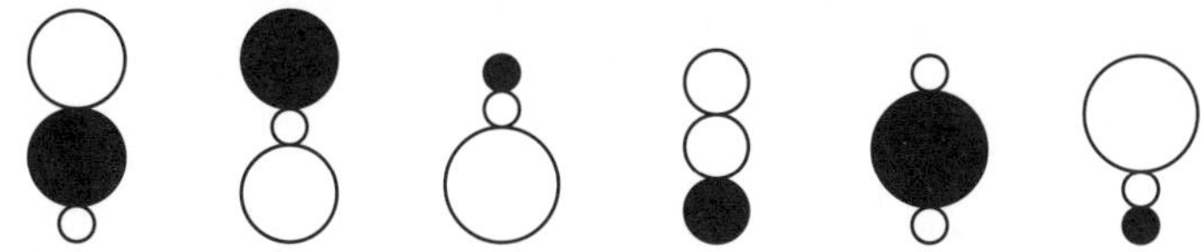

AY AX BX CZ BY **?**

BX AZ BZ CY CX

a **b** **c** **d** **e**

8

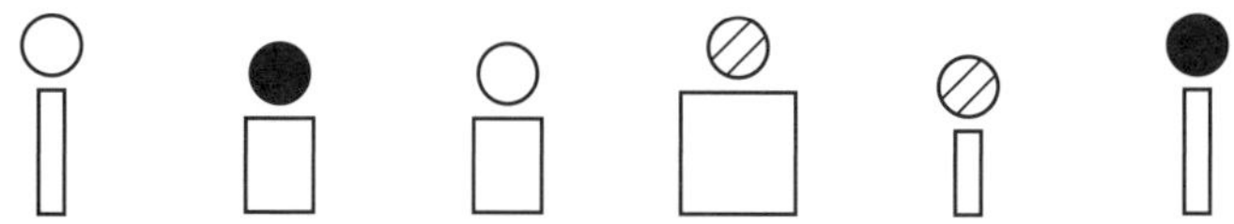

AX DZ DX BY CY **?**

CZ AZ BZ CX AY

a **b** **c** **d** **e**

9

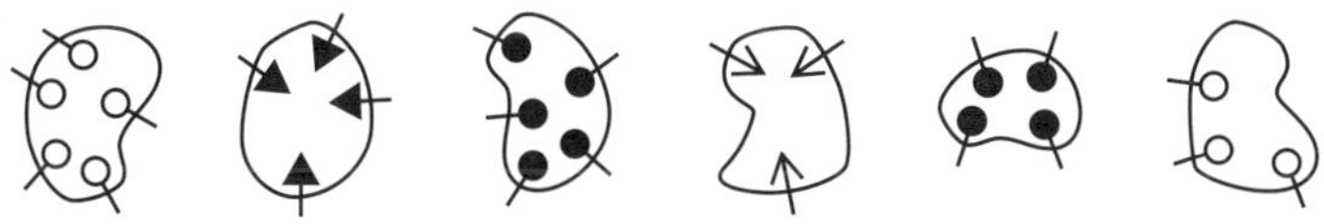

GU FV GT ES FT **?**

EU FU EV ET GV

a **b** **c** **d** **e**

Which cube could not be made from the given net?

10

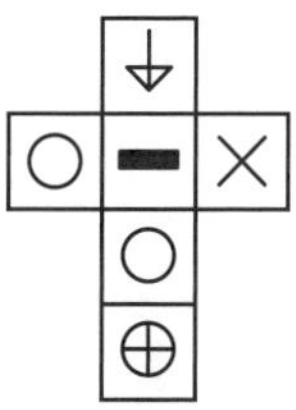

a **b** **c** **d** **e**

11

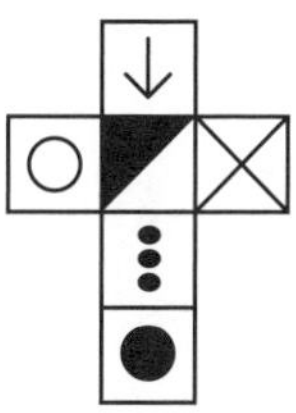

a **b** **c** **d** **e**

12

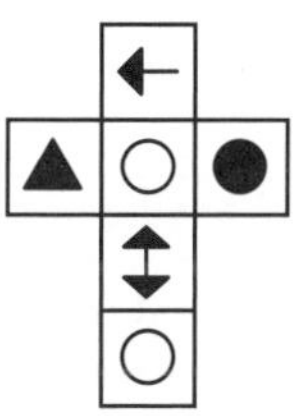

a **b** **c** **d** **e**

Total

Test 15: Mixed

Test time: 0 5 10 minutes

Which pattern continues or completes the given series?

1

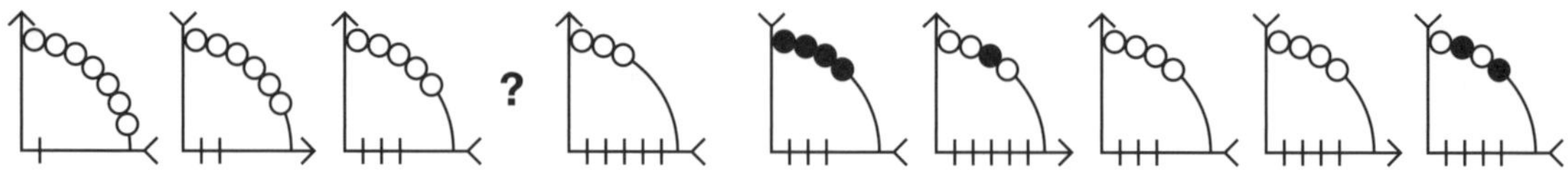

a b c d e

2

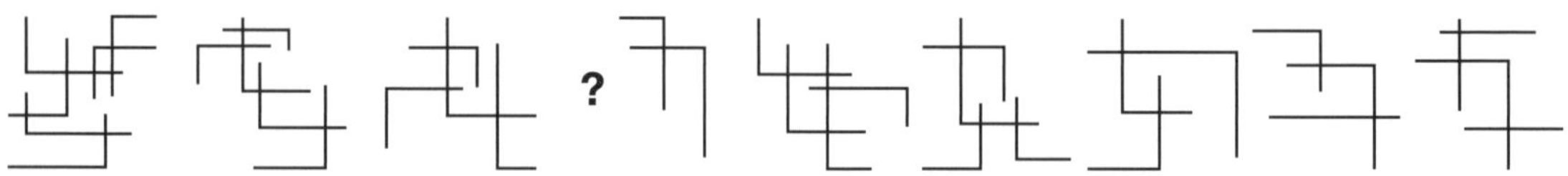

a b c d e

3

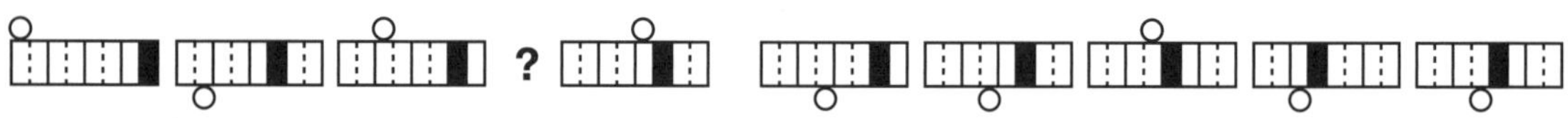

a b c d e

Using the given patterns and codes, select the code that matches the last pattern.

4

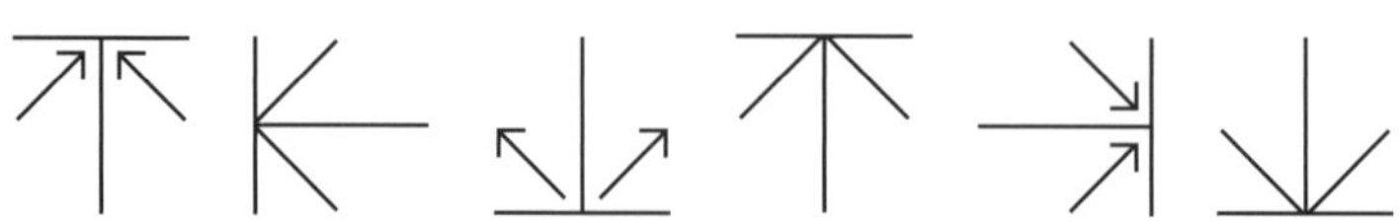

AX DZ CY AZ BX ?

DY CZ AY BZ CX
a b c d e

5

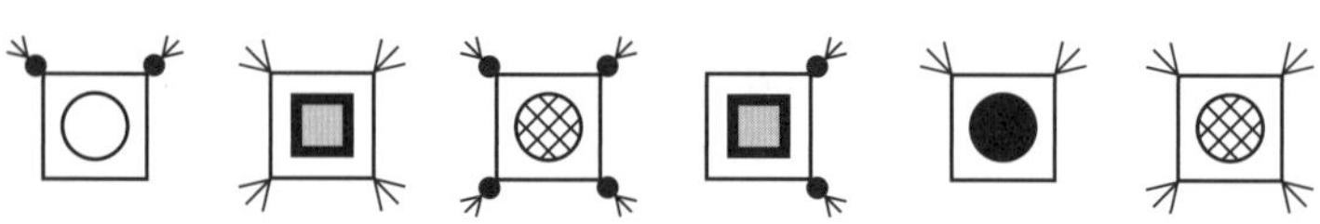

LS PV MT LV NU ?

PS PT LT NV MU
a b c d e

6

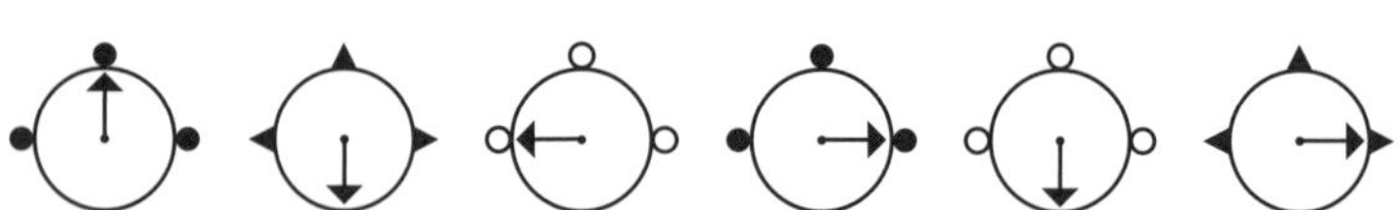

YB ZD XA YC XD ?

ZC XP YA XC ZB
a b c d e

In which of the patterns is the given shape hidden?

7
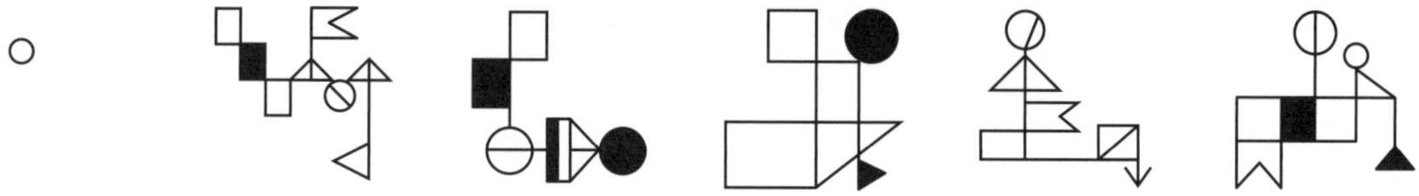
a b c d e

8
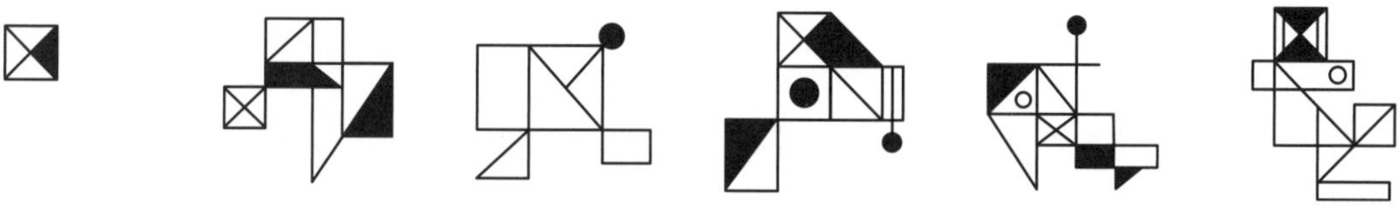
a b c d e

9
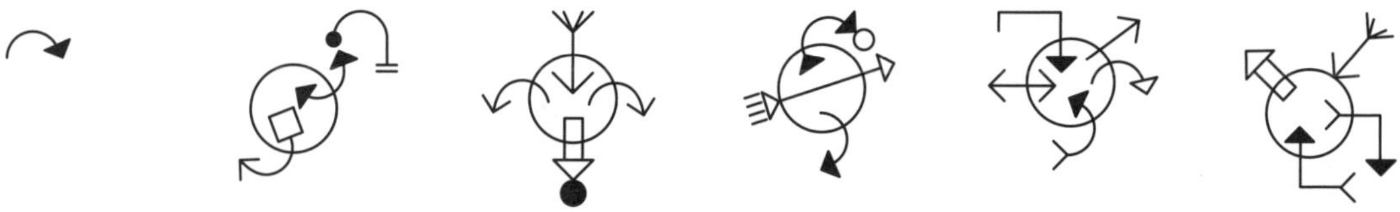
a b c d e

Which shape on the right goes best with the shapes on the left?

10

a b c d e

11
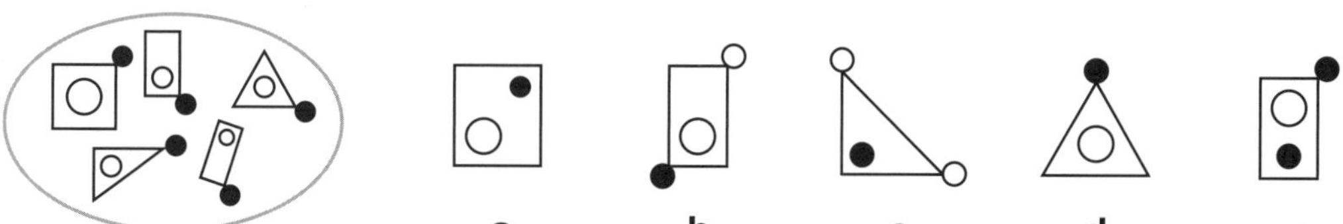
a b c d e

12
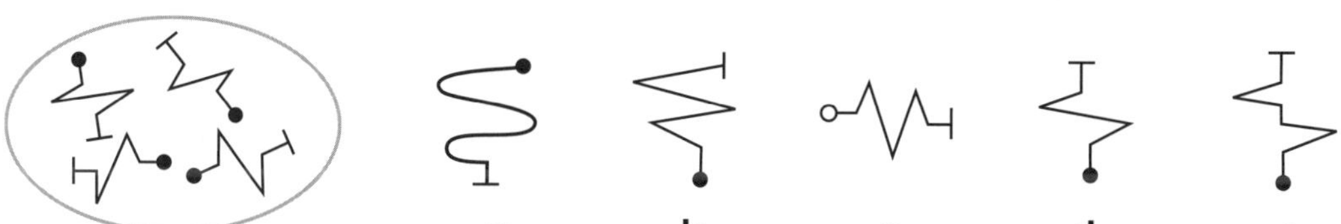
a b c d e

Total

Test 16: Mixed

Test time: 0 5 10 minutes

Which cube could not be made from the given net?

1

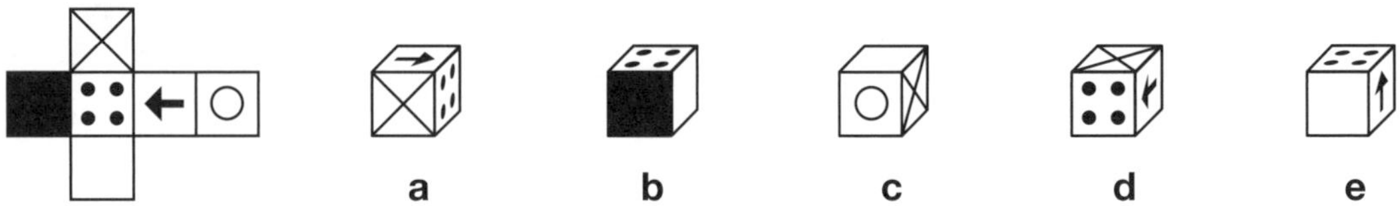

a b c d e

2

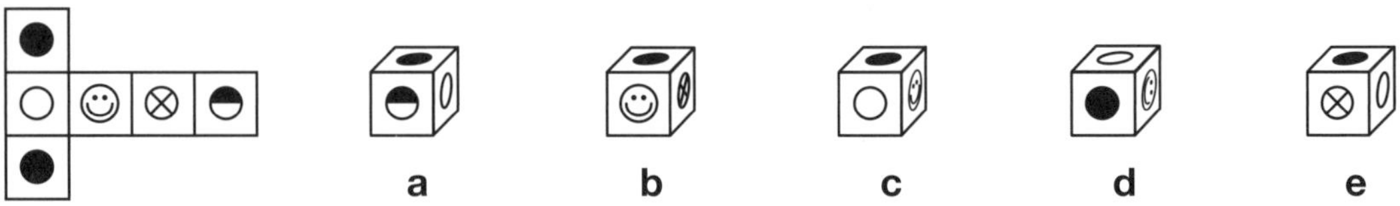

a b c d e

3

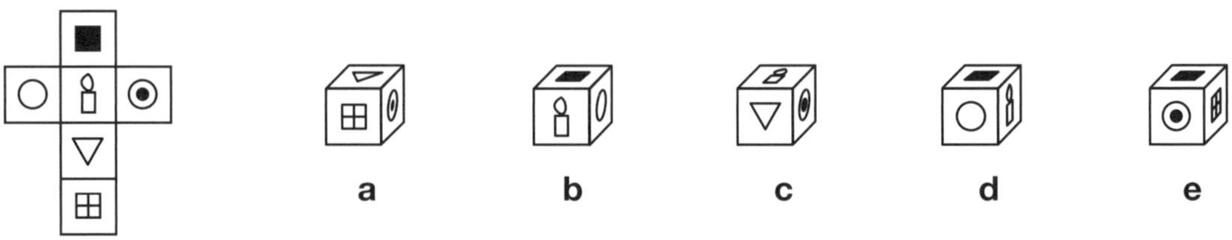

a b c d e

Which shape or pattern completes the second pair in the same way as the first pair?

4

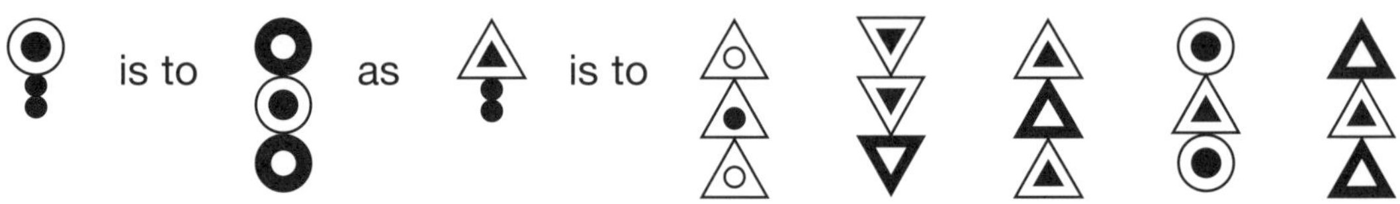

a b c d e

5

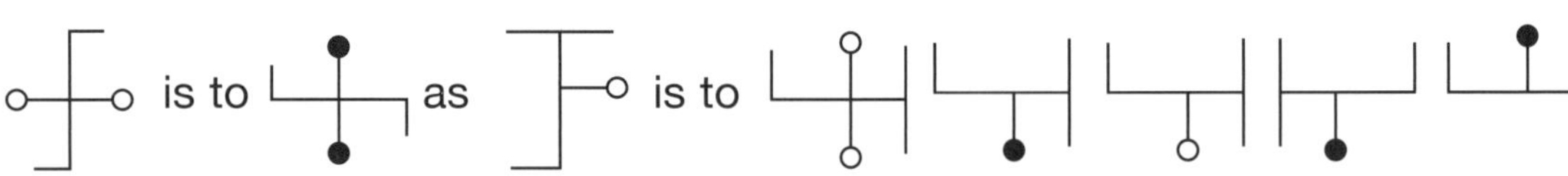

a b c d e

6

a b c d e

Which shape on the right goes best with the shapes on the left?

7

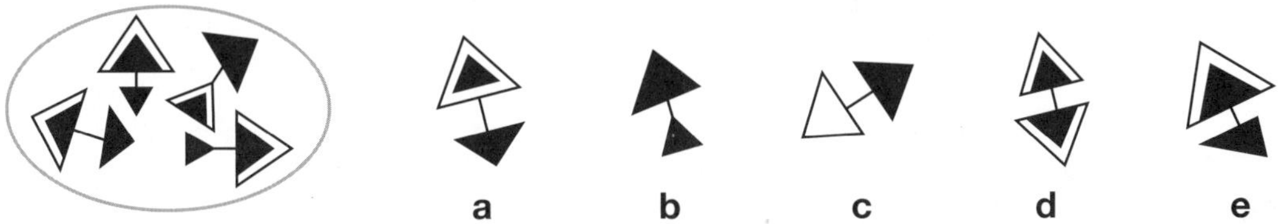

8

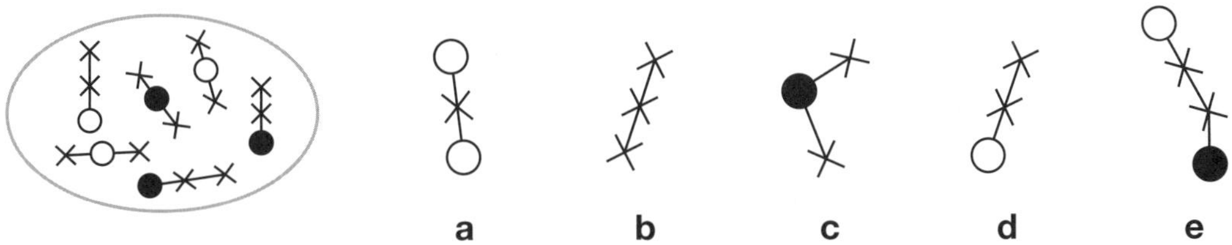

9

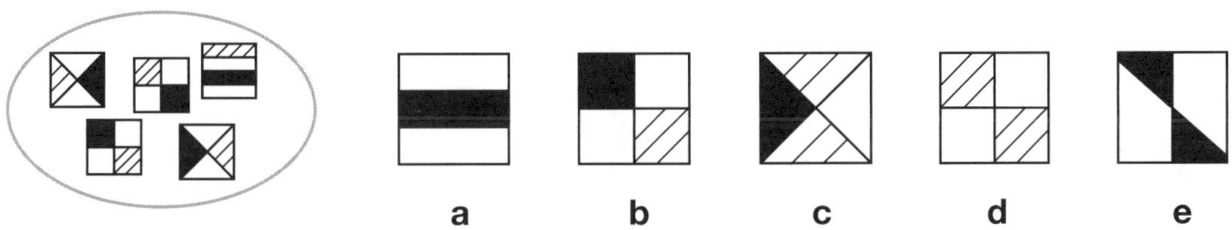

Which is the mirror image of the shape on the left?

10

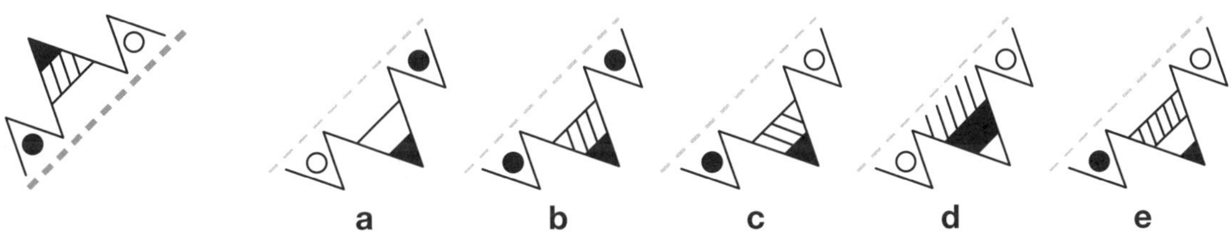

11

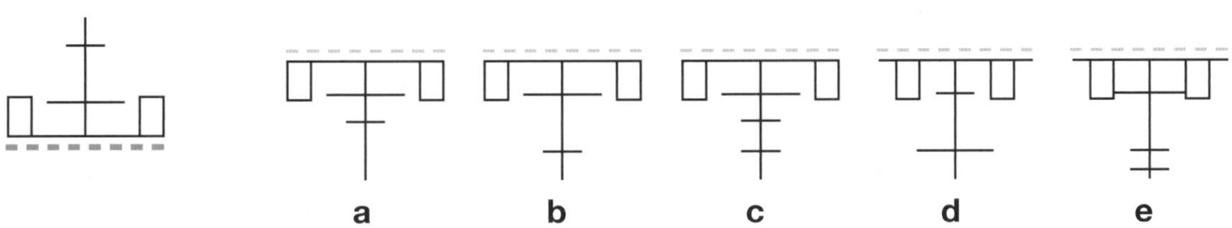

12

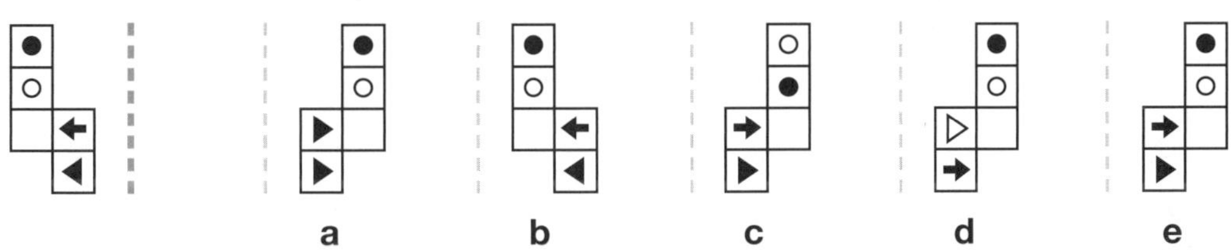

Time for a break! Go to Puzzle Page 45

Total

Test 17: Mixed

Test time: 0 5 10 minutes

Using the given patterns and codes, select the code that matches the last pattern.

1

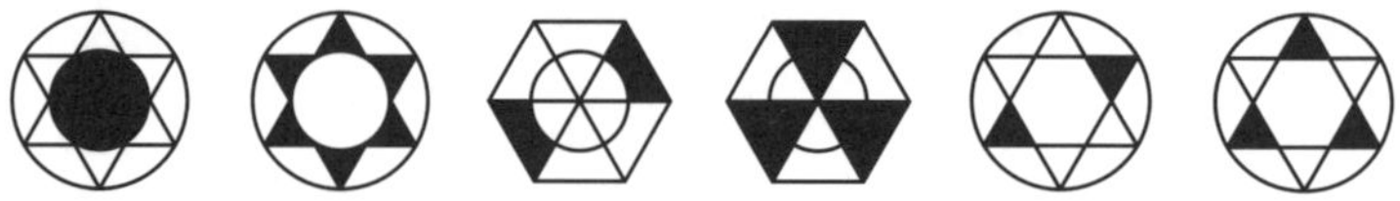

AX DX BY CY BX ?

DY BX CX BY CY
a **b** **c** **d** **e**

2

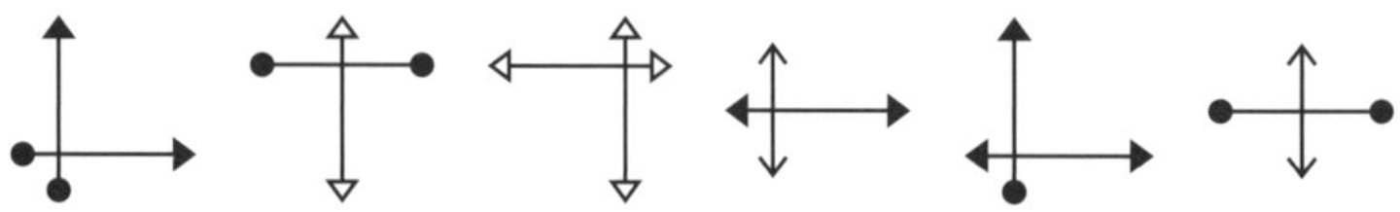

AS BV BU CT AT ?

CU BT AU CV AV
a **b** **c** **d** **e**

3

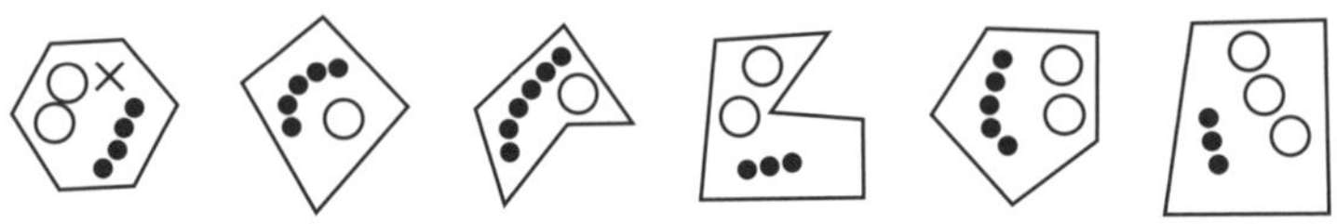

NB LC MD NA MC ?

MA LA ND NC LB
a **b** **c** **d** **e**

Which shape or pattern completes the second pair in the same way as the first pair?

4

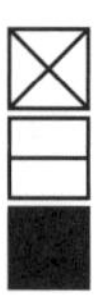 is to  as  is to

a **b** **c** **d** **e**

5

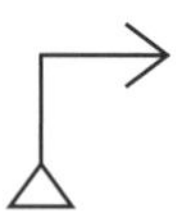 is to  as  is to

a **b** **c** **d** **e**

6

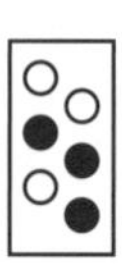 is to 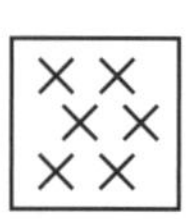 as  is to

a **b** **c** **d** **e**

Which pattern continues or completes the given series?

7
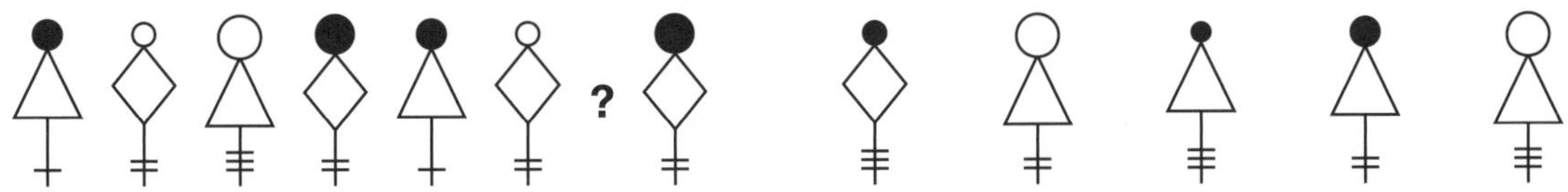
a b c d e

8
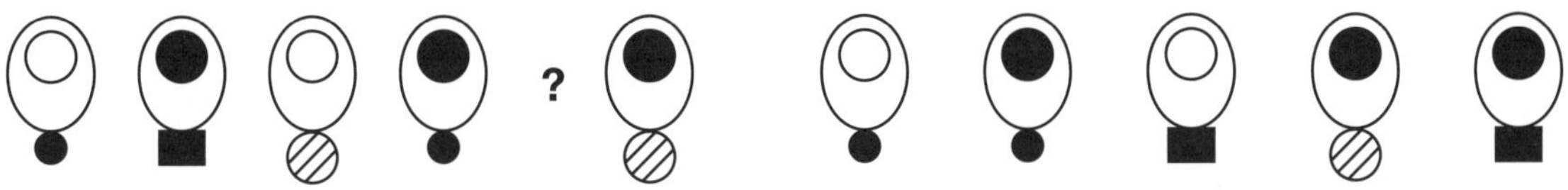
a b c d e

9
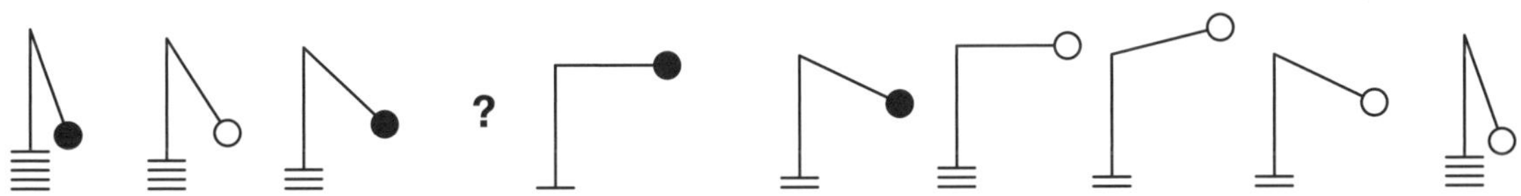
a b c d e

Which shape on the right goes best with the shapes on the left?

10
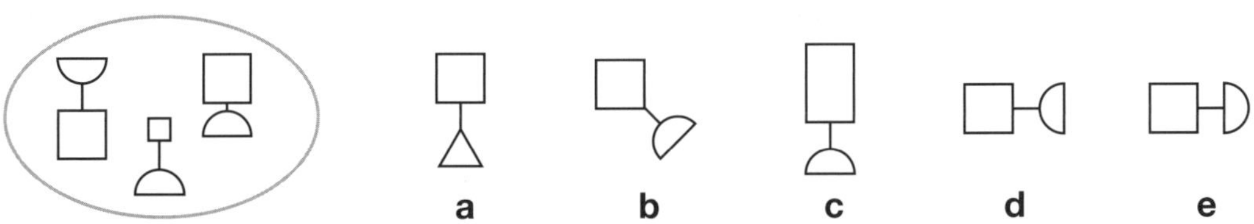
a b c d e

11

a b c d e

12

a b c d e

Total

Test 18: Mixed

Test time: 0 5 10 minutes

Using the given patterns and codes, select the code that matches the last pattern.

1

AY BZ CZ AX DY ?

CY CX BY AZ DX
a **b** **c** **d** **e**

2

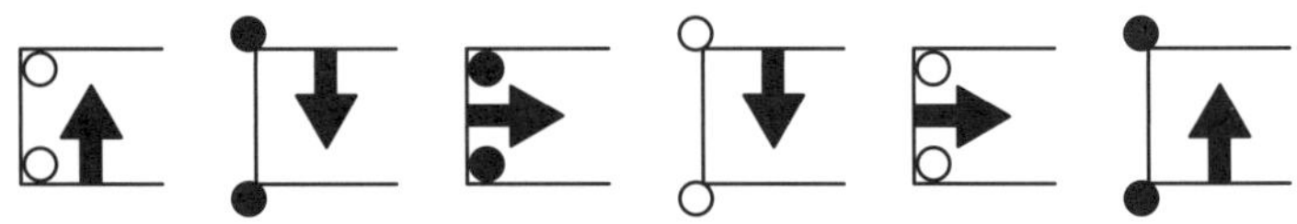

FP HS GR HQ GP ?

GQ HP FS HR FR
a **b** **c** **d** **e**

3

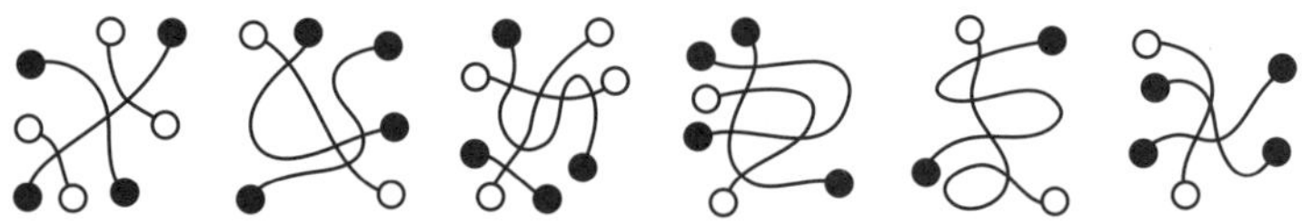

AJ BK AM BL CK ?

BM AK CJ BJ CL
a **b** **c** **d** **e**

Which shape or pattern completes the second pair in the same way as the first pair?

4

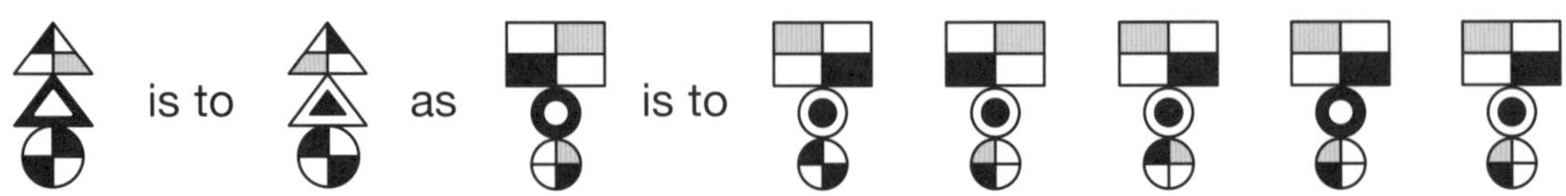

a **b** **c** **d** **e**

5

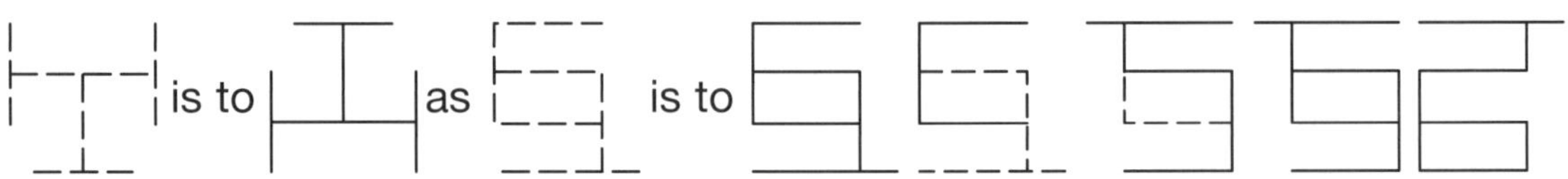

a **b** **c** **d** **e**

6

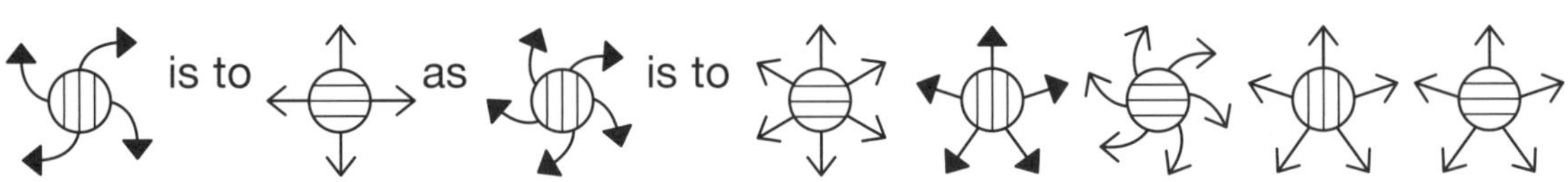

a **b** **c** **d** **e**

Which pattern continues or completes the given series?

7

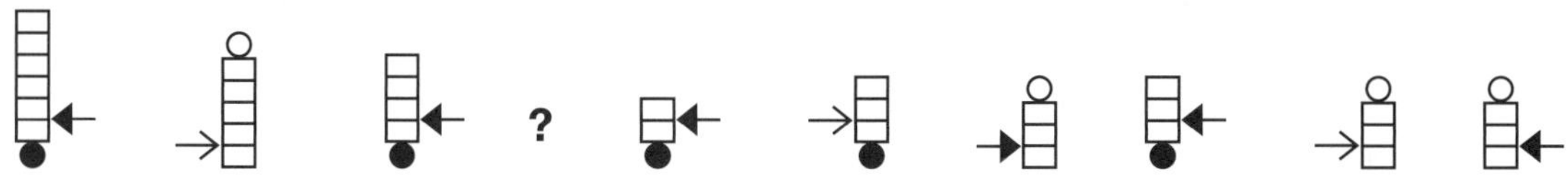

a b c d e

8

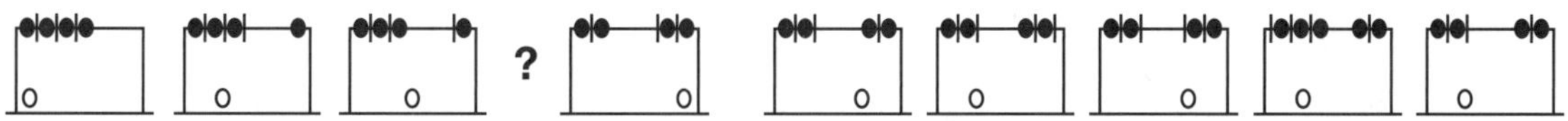

a b c d e

9

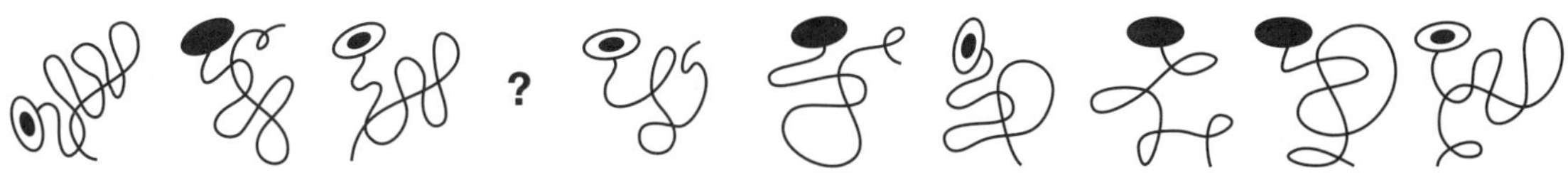

a b c d e

Which cube could not be made from the given net?

10

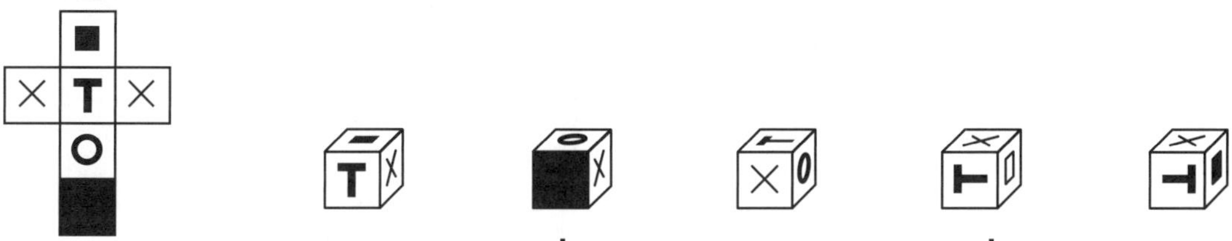

a b c d e

11

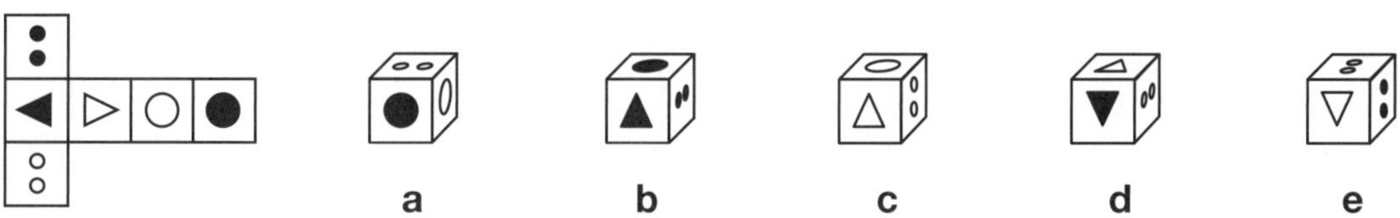

a b c d e

12

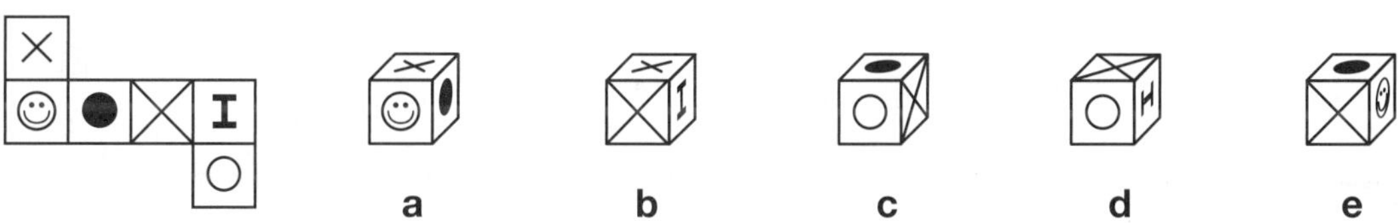

a b c d e

Total

Test 19: Mixed

Test time: 0 5 10 minutes

Which shape on the right goes best with the shapes on the left?

1 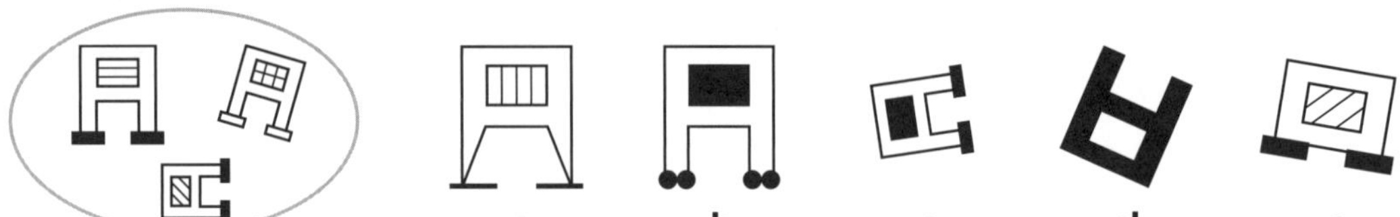

a b c d e

2 

a b c d e

3 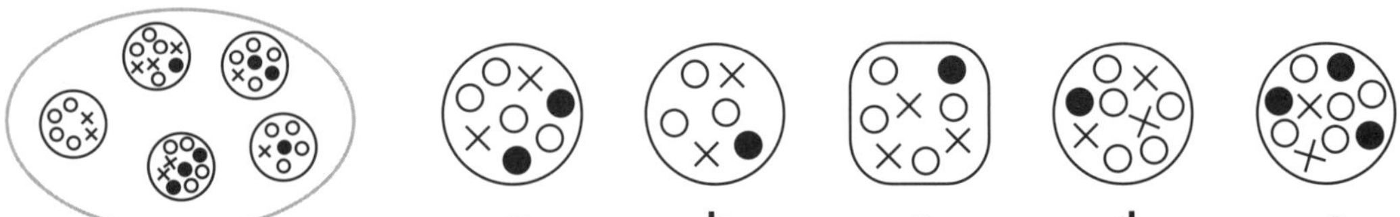

a b c d e

4 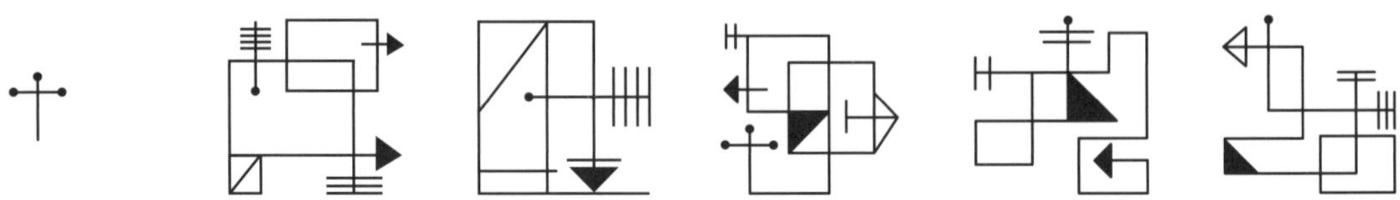

a b c d e

5 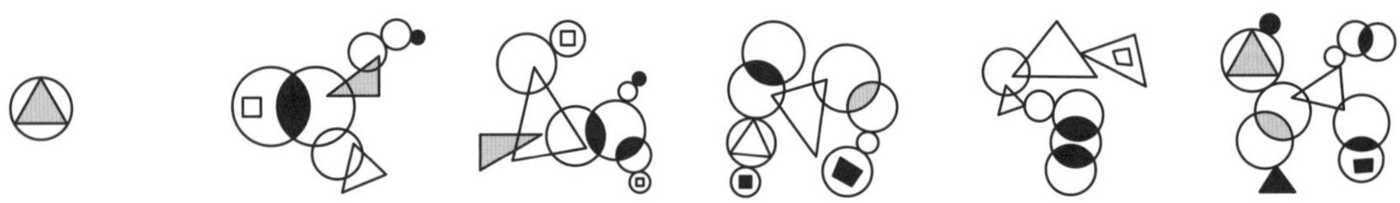

a b c d e

6 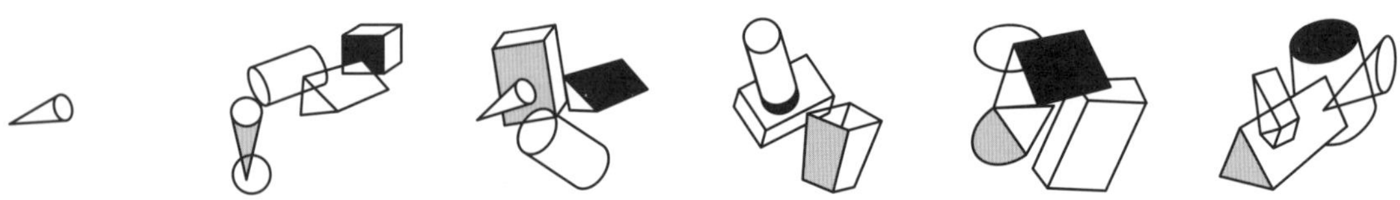

a b c d e

Using the given patterns and codes, select the code that matches the last pattern.

7

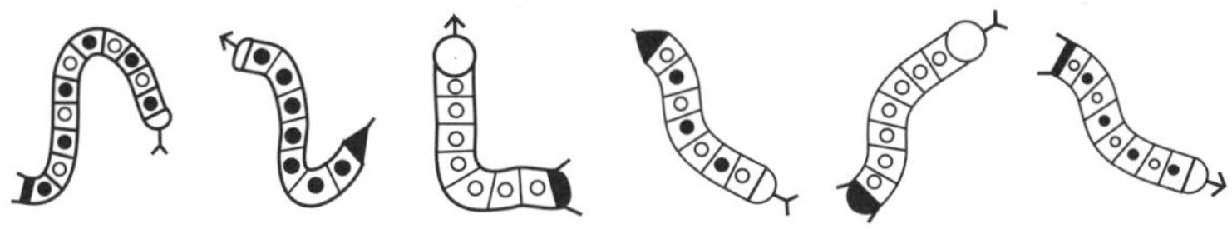

AZ BX CY AX DY ?

a	b	c	d	e
BY	BZ	AY	CZ	CX

8

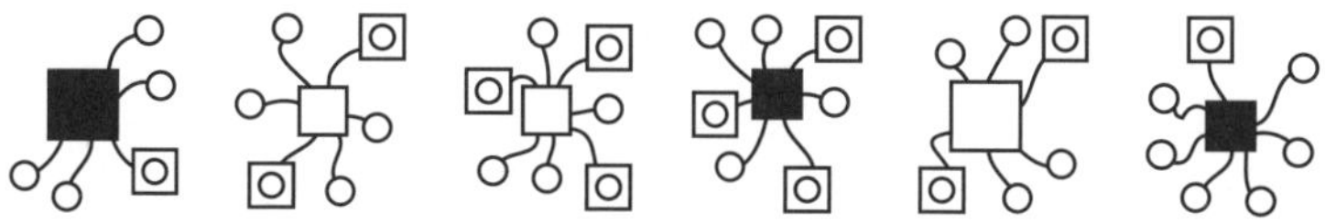

EX HY HZ GZ FY ?

a	b	c	d	e
GX	FZ	HX	EY	GY

9

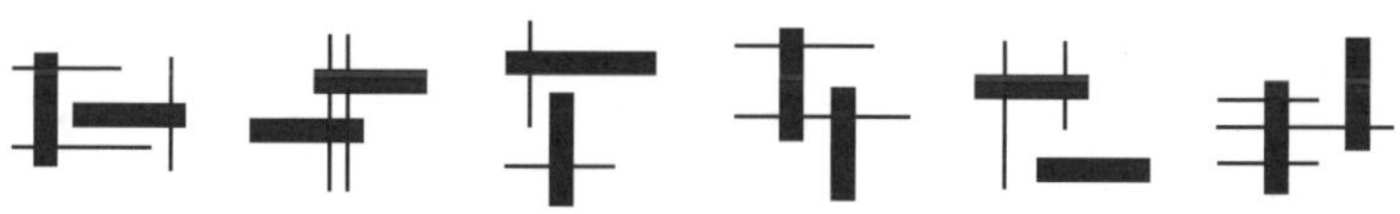

AY BZ AX CY BX ?

a	b	c	d	e
CX	BY	AY	AZ	CZ

Which is the mirror image of the shape on the left?

10

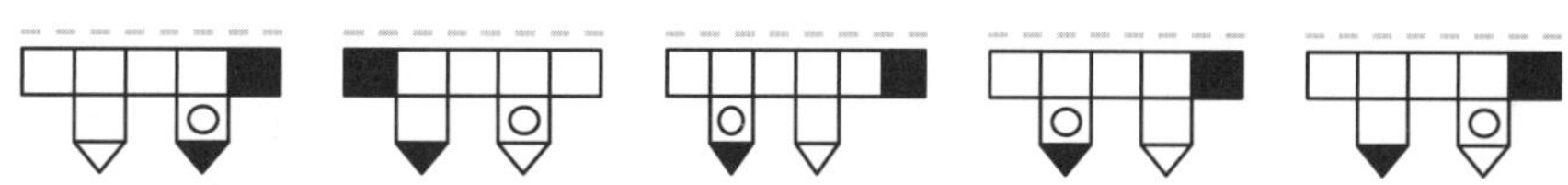

a b c d e

11

a b c d e

12

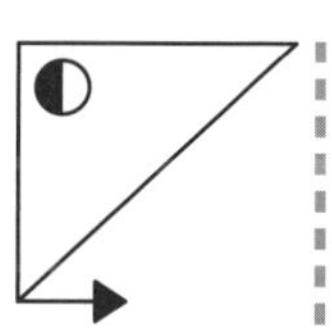

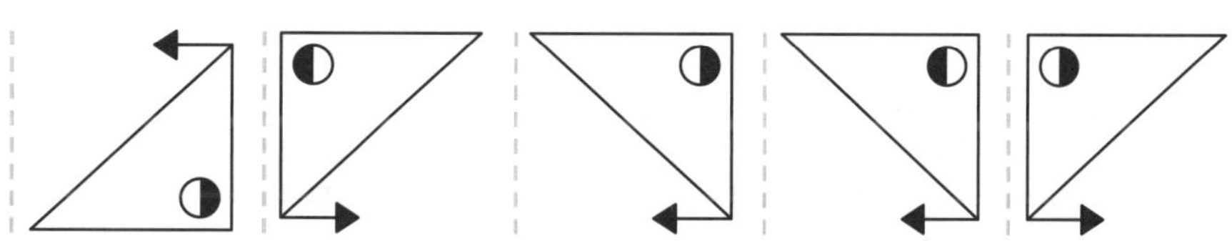

a b c d e

Total

TEST 20: Mixed

Test time: 0 5 10 minutes

Which pattern continues or completes the given series or grid?

1

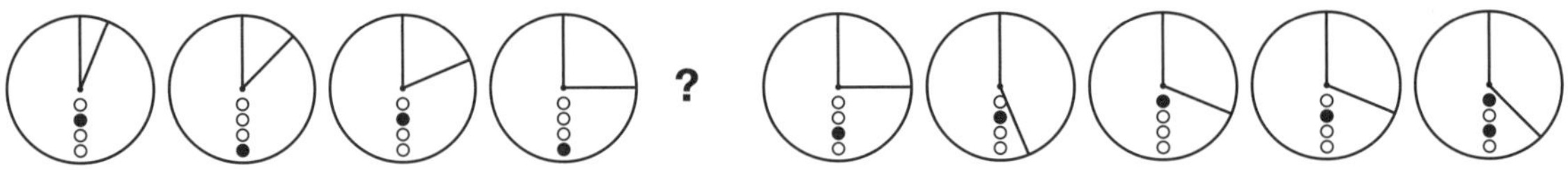

a b c d e

2

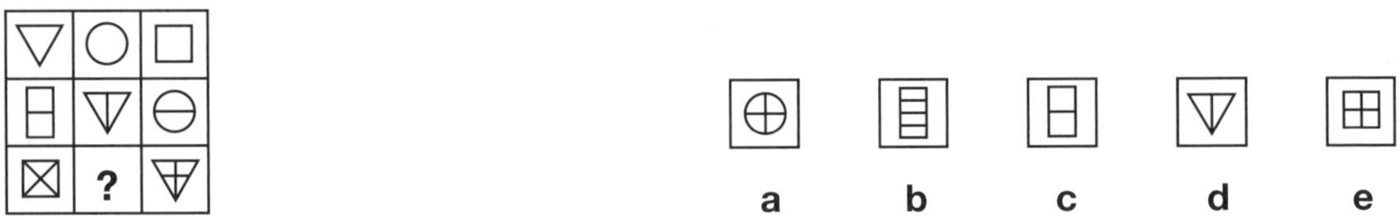

a b c d e

3

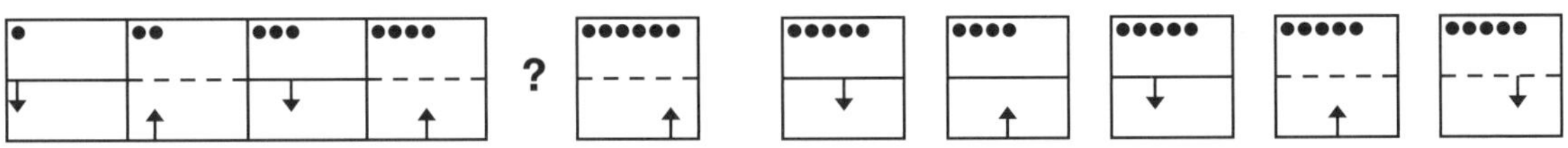

a b c d e

Which shape or pattern completes the second pair in the same way as the first pair?

4

a b c d e

5

a b c d e

6

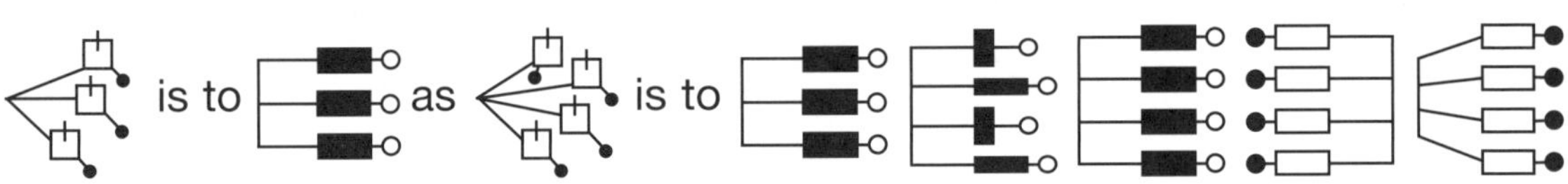

a b c d e

Which cube could not be made from the given net?

7
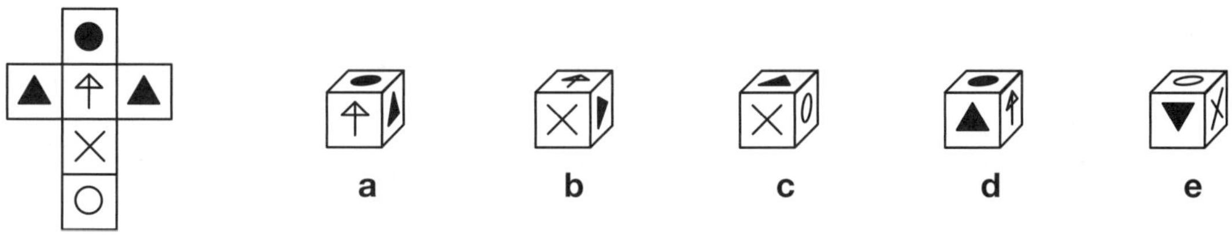
a b c d e

8
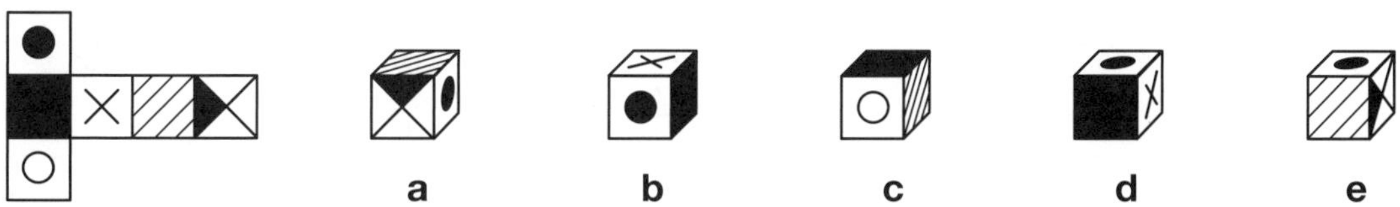
a b c d e

9
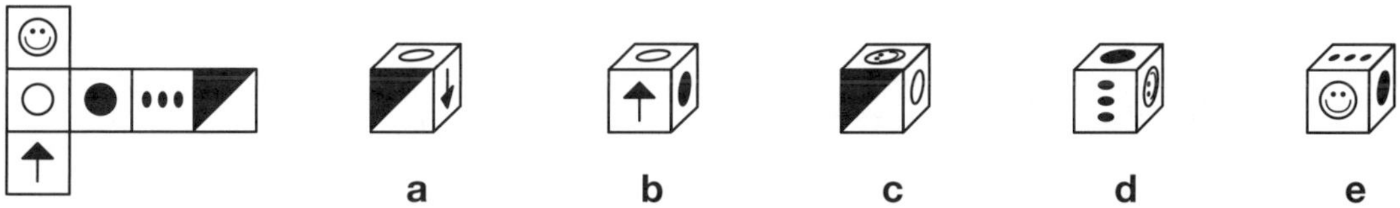
a b c d e

Which shape on the right goes best with the shapes on the left?

10
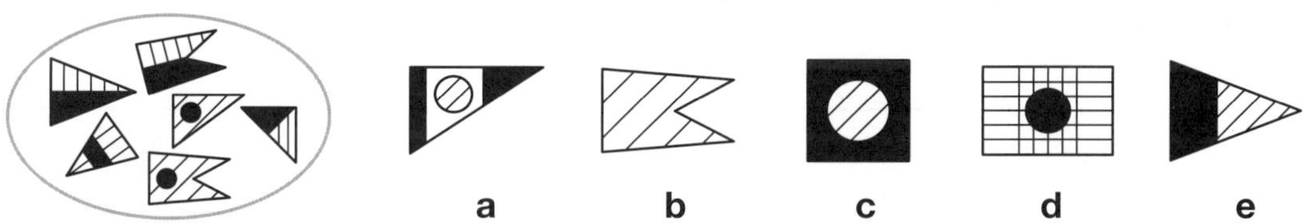
a b c d e

11
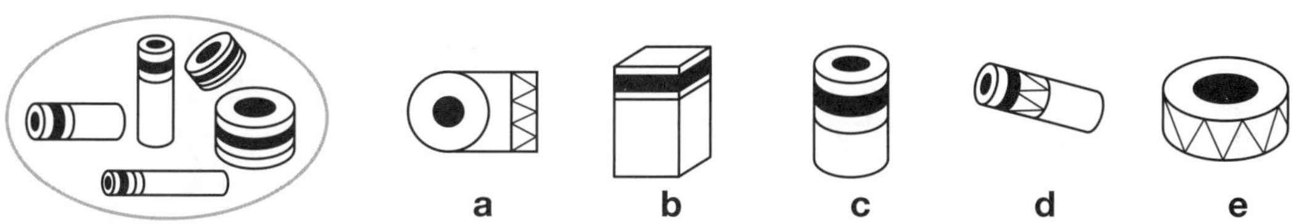
a b c d e

12
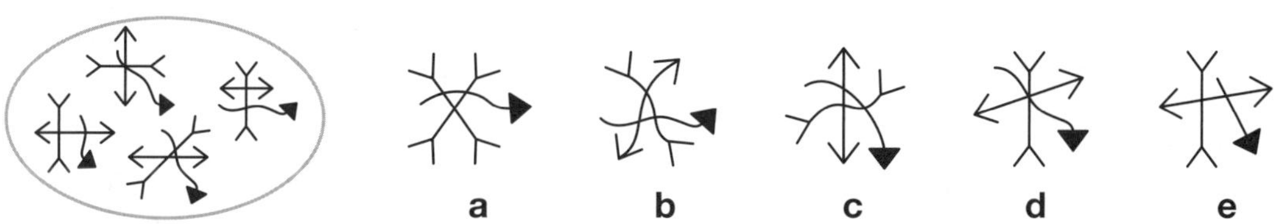
a b c d e

Time for a break! Go to Puzzle Page 46

Total

Puzzle 1

Circle the two sets of parallel lines that are not equal in length.

A

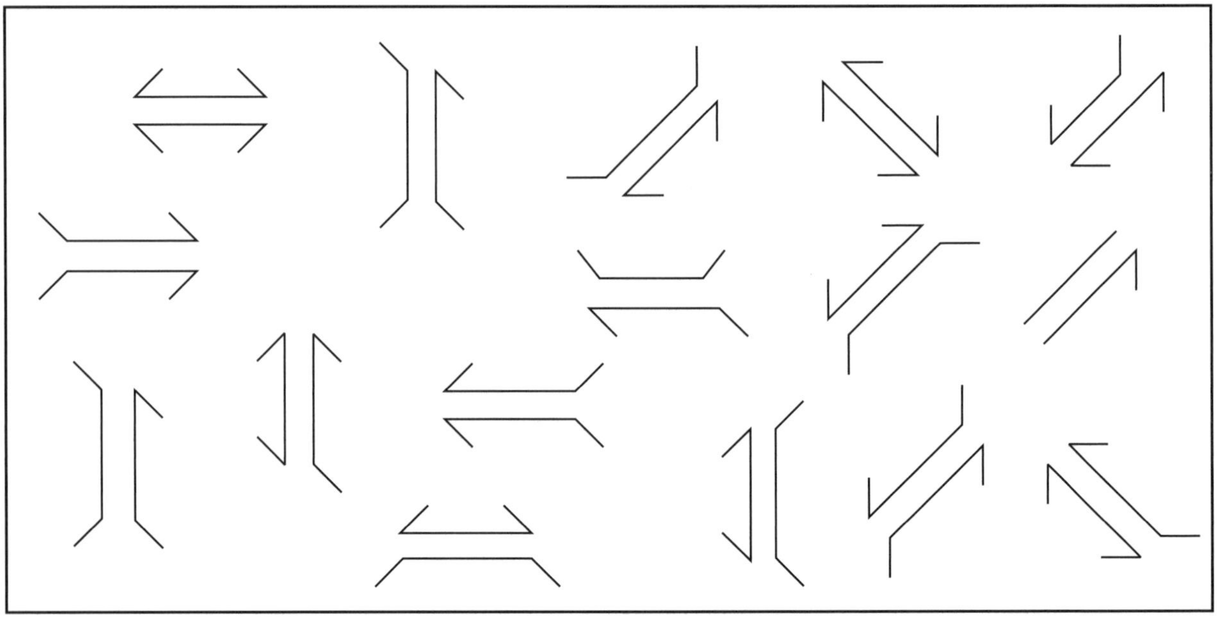

In which pattern is the bold square bigger than the white square in the middle.

B

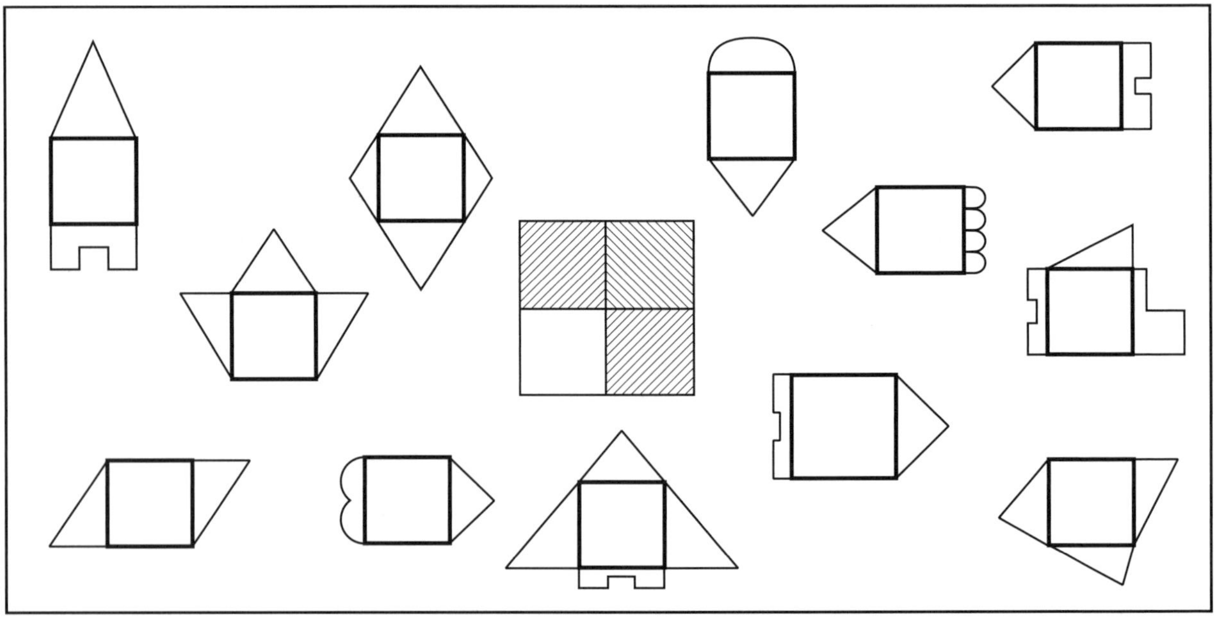

Puzzle ❷

In each box circle the pattern that is different from the rest.

A

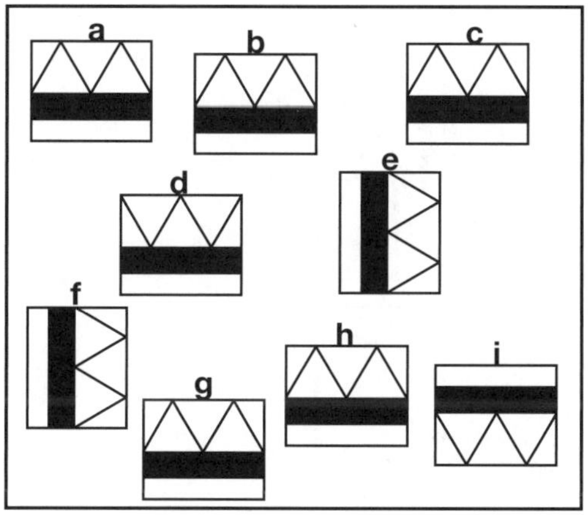

B

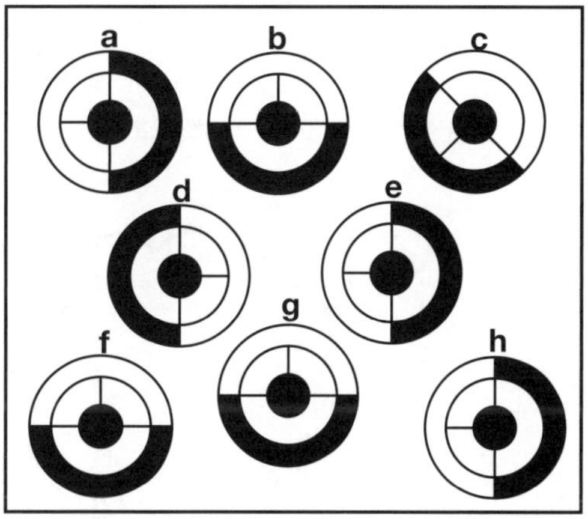

C

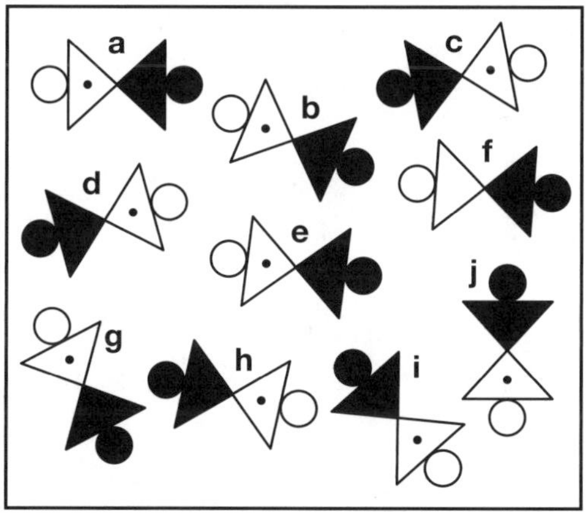

D

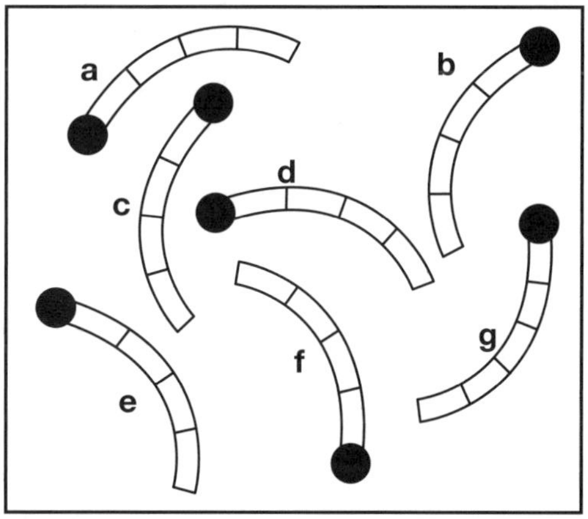

E

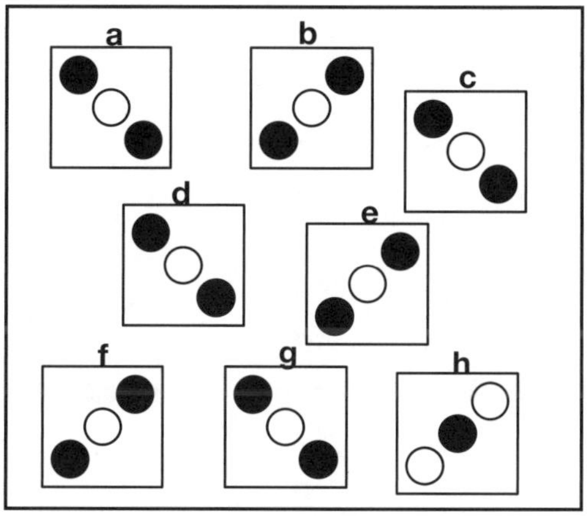

F

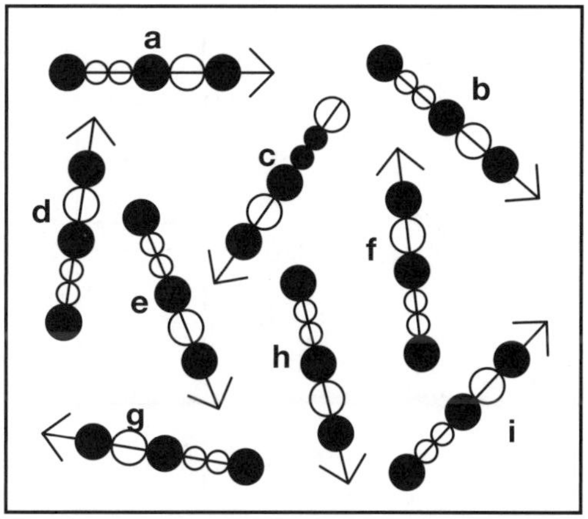

Puzzle ❸

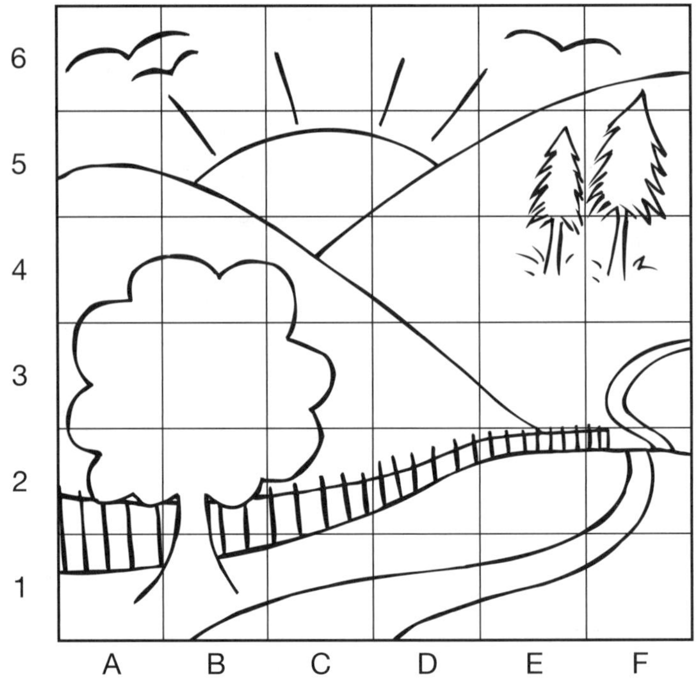

Which grid square is drawn below?

A

A3	B4	C3	C4
a	**b**	**c**	**d**

B

B6	C4	F1	F6
a	**b**	**c**	**d**

C

C2	E2	D2	A2
a	**b**	**c**	**d**

D

F6	C5	A5	D1
a	**b**	**c**	**d**

E

C6	F1	E4	D6
a	**b**	**c**	**d**

F

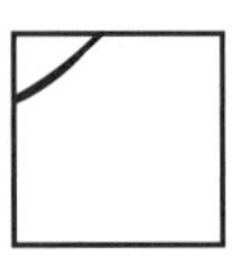

F3	F1	C2	C4
a	**b**	**c**	**d**

Puzzle 4

Identify and link the shapes that form a pair, in the same way as the pair already joined.

A

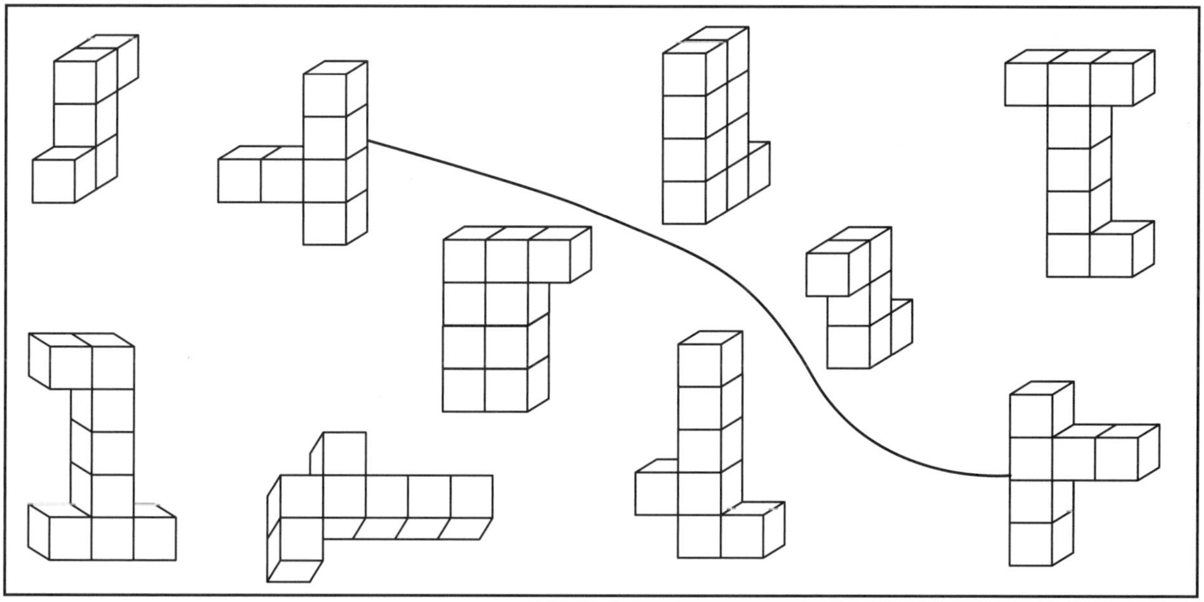

Join each shape on the left with its mirror image on the right.

B

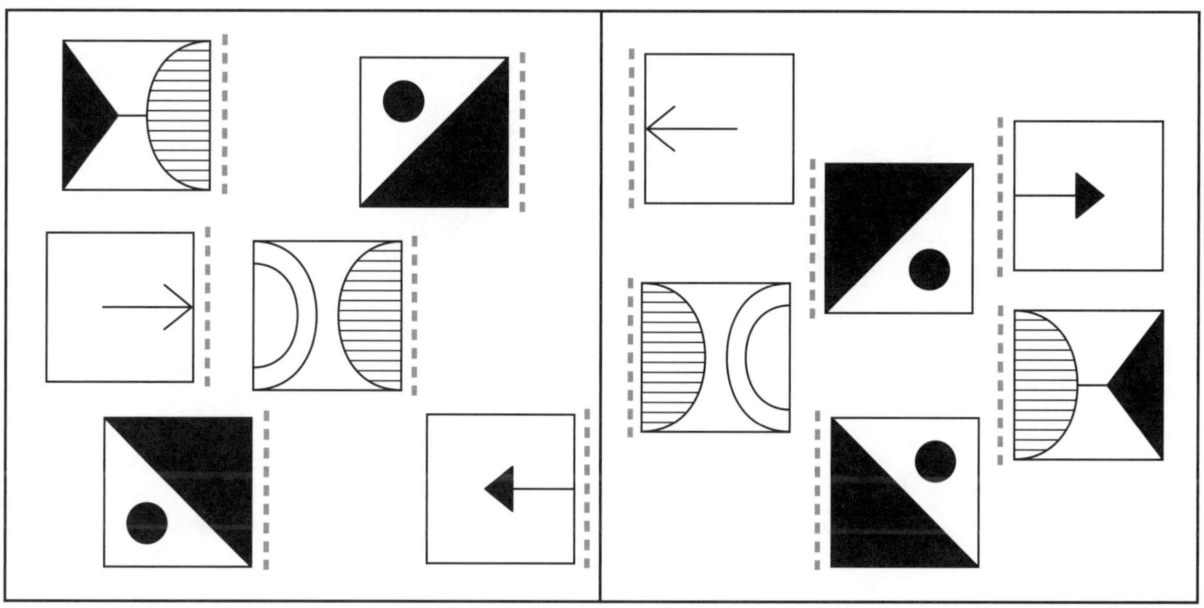

Puzzle ❺

Complete these patterns by drawing their reflection in the dotted mirror line.
The first one has been started for you:

A

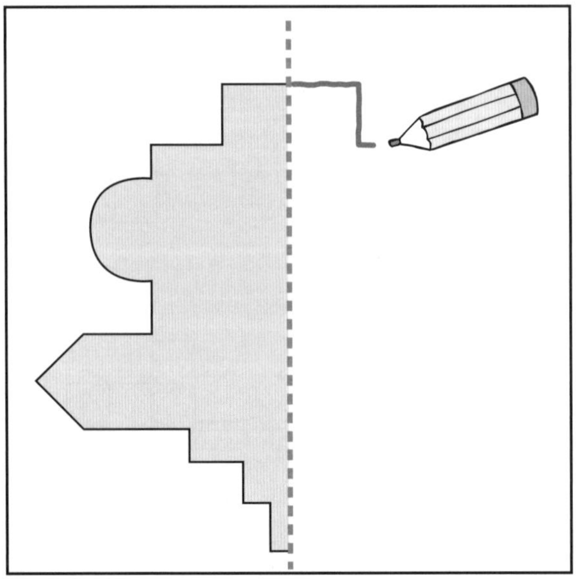

B

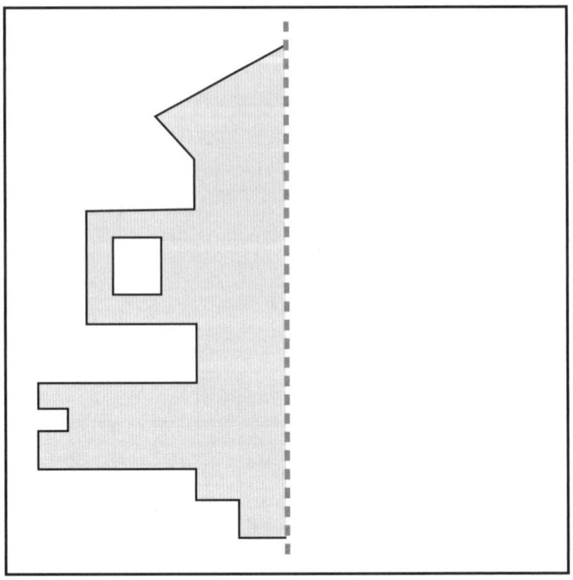

C

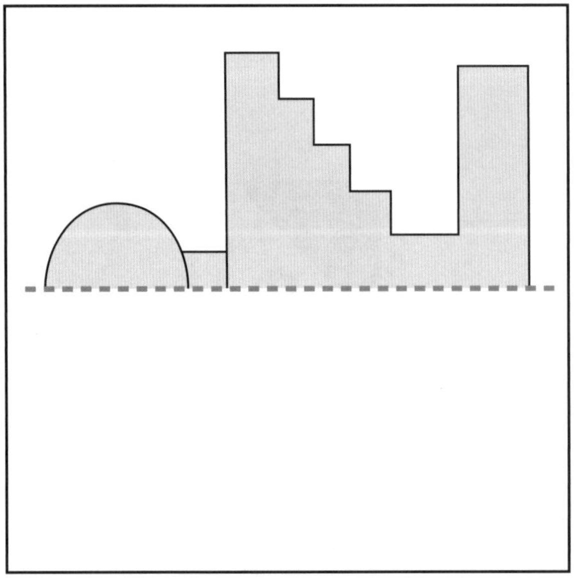

D

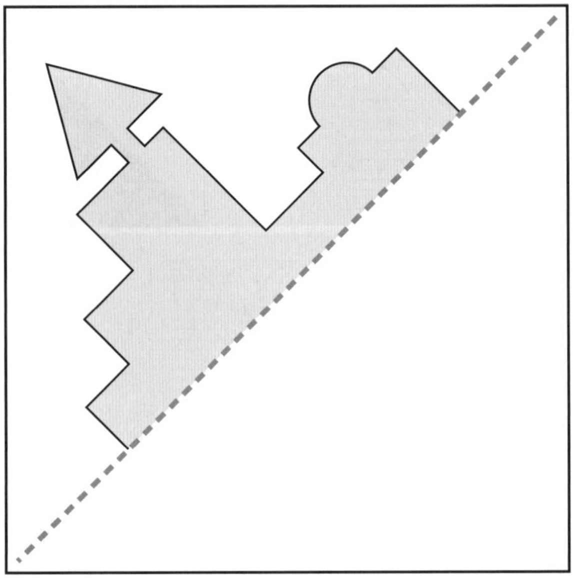

Progress Grid Non-verbal Reasoning 10 Minute Tests 10–11+ years

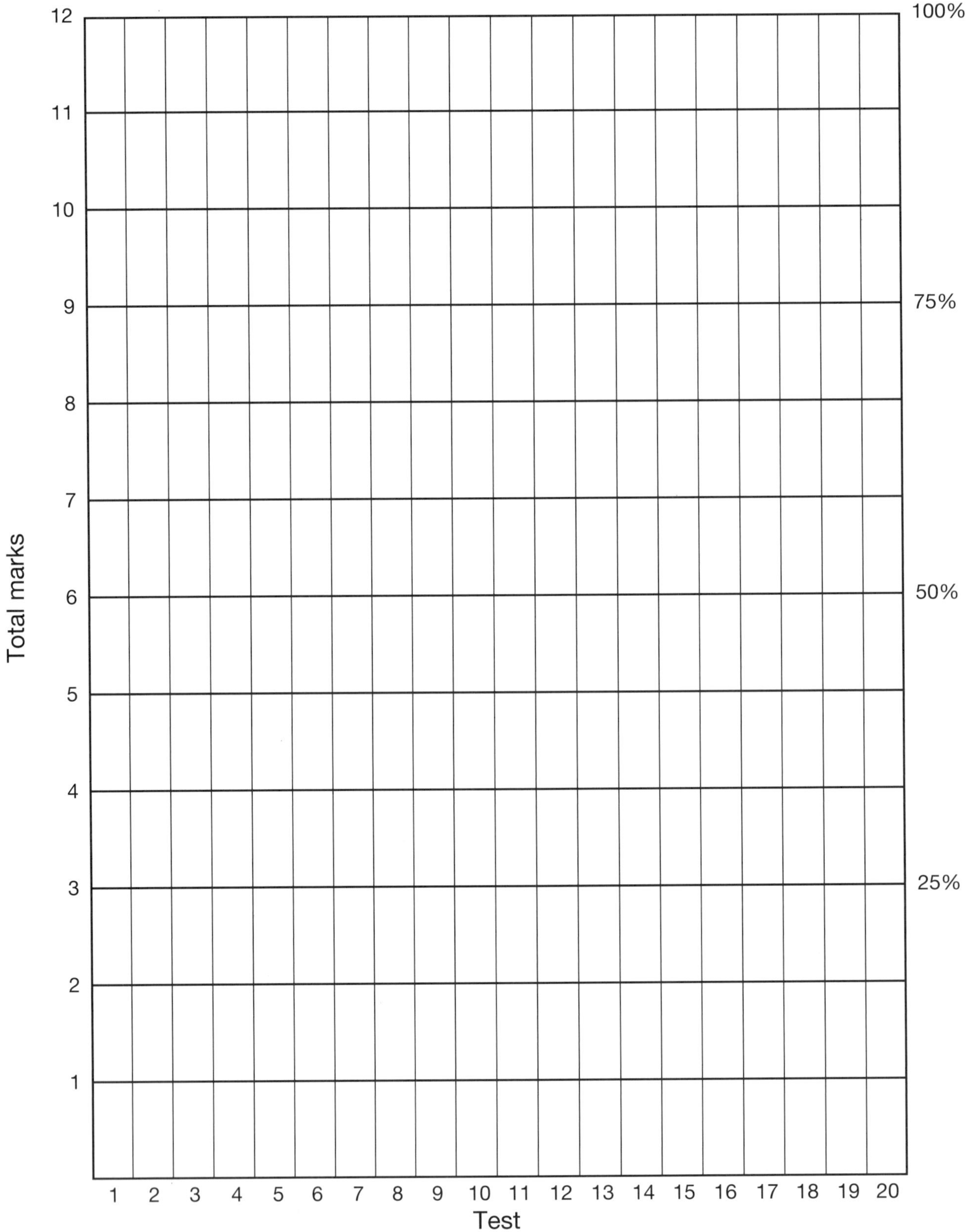